STOCK OPTIONS
TRADING FOR BEGINNERS

THE ULTIMATE GUIDE FOR STOCK MARKET
INVESTING&TRADING
FOR BEGINNERS
INVESTING IN THE STOCK MARKET
FOR BEGINNERS

Dennis Read

WRITTEN BY:

DENNIS READ

Table of Contents

Introduction

Stocks are a form of investment or specifically—securities that will give you a portion of the company as in you can get the ownership of a certain part of the company—also known as shares. But what will you do with stocks? Well, as an investor, you can buy the stocks when you speculate that their price is going to increase. And when the increase in price happens, you can then sell the stocks and bring home profits. Anyone who purchases stocks becomes the shareholder of that particular company because they own a part of that company. They also get to share the profits.

Some people think that it is only the private companies that have shareholders, but that is a wrong concept. Both private and public companies have stocks, and thus both of them have shareholders too.

It requires only a small group of people to form a business, but in order to get more cash for the business, companies go public and sell their stocks. This is when people buy their stocks, and they get the money. No matter how many investors have invested in the stocks, every investor will be getting their share of the profit when the company performs well. But at the same time, if the performance of the company is poor, then the investors will hold an equal risk of losing money.

Start investing and studying the market. Start by studying the market and doing some paper trading in your free time. This will allow you to practice trading without the risk of losing money. It also allows you to test out your preferred investment strategies.

While learning about the stock market, you will often find yourself overwhelmed by all the information in the market. You will need to keep tabs on all your target companies and the companies that you are already invested in. It is understandable to feel overwhelmed.

To keep everything organized, start a journal for your investing activities and thoughts. One way to do this is by putting all your decisions and your reasons behind them in your journal. This will allow you to keep track of all of the strategies that you use. It will allow you to keep track of the strategies that do work.

Make it a habit to read your own journal entries. This is one of the best ways to learn from your own triumphs and mistakes. The investors in the world remember many of their trades. They learn from their past mistakes and, if needed, they adjust their behavior to make sure these mistakes are not repeated.

Losses are inevitable when investing in the stock market. It does not matter if you lose money every now and then. It's impossible to be right all the time. You need to make sure though, that you do not lose more money than you gain. You can do this by making sure that each of your buying decisions is based on sound analysis.

CHAPTER 1:

Stock Options Trading for Beginners

Getting Started

B efore signing up to any investment platform or spending a dime, you would like to know the most vital step to getting started and staying successful while trading. That step is learning. At this stage in your life, you have time. You don't have to jump in immediately. It's far better to take at least a few weeks, preferably a month or more, to find out as much as you can about investing. Inspect every book from the library (a resource section including recommended books are going to be included), watch tutorials, and skim news about the market. Watch the investing shows Mad Money and Squawk on the road. Experts like Jim Cramer recommend investors spend one hour per week researching each stock that they own or want to take a position in, so continuous learning may be a lifelong process for a sensible investor. On top of all that, confirm to possess an honest understanding of the stock exchange literacy section later in this book. Learning as much as possible will prevent money down the road and is completely instrumental while choosing good stocks and truly making money. The next step to be put into action, either in your learning period or afterward, is to open a virtual portfolio. Virtual portfolios are portfolios that allow you to take a position of virtual money in real stocks at real market values.

Opening an Actual Account

Once you've learned as much as you'll and you understand the fundamentals of investing and picking stocks, it is time to open an actual investment account so you'll start trading for real. Opening an account is harder for minors than adults and requires the help of a guardian. Accounts for minors are called custodial accounts. These accounts allow the minor to legally trade (instead of just trading under the parent's name) and have several benefits. Custodial accounts are taxed at a lower rate, even 0% on much of the initial gains, rather than the standard adult rates. (This varies by case.) Custodial accounts automatically transfer ownership to the minor once they reach a particular age, either 18 or 21. Many platforms offer custodial accounts and in this section, the pros and cons of the best programs are going to be discussed.

E*TRADE—etrade.com

E*TRADE is the most established and one among the oldest online brokers, with an extended history that spans from 1982 to this date. E*TRADE is the platform that I started with and currently use, and offers mutual funds, stocks, and options for

$0 commissions alongside a full range of research and analyst tools. Custodial users get their own login.

Charles Schwab—schwab.com

Charles Schwab is one of the most important investment firms in the world and offers $0 commission trades alongside a good range of research tools. They provide custodial accounts that use an equivalent login as an existing guardian's account. Thereupon being said, if your guardian uses this service and doesn't want you to remember their financial situation, this platform isn't for you. If that doesn't apply to you, Charles Schwab is one of the best all-around options.

Stockpile—stockpile.com

Stockpile is an investment platform designed specifically for teenagers. It offers custodial accounts on an easy and youth-friendly interface in which users can purchase fractional shares in large companies. The downsides are that Stockpile only offers 1,000 approximately of the most important American companies rather than the complete market and takes a 99 cent commission per trade. Stockpile has introductory lessons on investing and allows for stock "wish lists" to be sent. Overall, it's an honest option for somebody trying to find a simplified option. An almost identical platform is Loved at loved.com.

TD Ameritrade—tdameritrade.com

TD Ameritrade may be a platform that's designed for users with experience and offers access to a number of the best research tools on the market.

Custodial accounts take $0 commissions and have offer custodial accounts with attention on saving for school.

Fidelity—fidelity.com

Fidelity's platform offers a full range of research tools alongside available investment analysis from experts in the field. They provide custodial accounts with $0 commissions, no fees, and no minimum balance. Overall, Fidelity is an all-around decent alternative for active investors.

Vanguard—vanguard.com

Vanguard is one of the most important brokerage services in the world and offers custodial accounts with $0 commissions and no fees. Vanguard's focus and specialty are Mutual Funds and ETFs, which make the platform better fitted to long-term and dividend investors.

Making Your First Investment

You ought to have decided which platform you would like to take a position with. Together with your parent's assistance, you'll start the method of opening an account. You're able to start investing real money into the important market and to do that, you would like money itself. Attempt to gather at least a few hundred dollars to start out, but far more importantly attempt to consistently add money. Remember the lesson on interest in the benefits section, and confine in mind that each dollar you invest today is going to be worth exponentially more in the future. To assist you out if you're trying to find some extra cash to take a position, let's re-evaluate 5 of the best ways to make money as an adolescent, all of which I can personally vouch for.

How to Monitor Your Investment Portfolio?

Before you start investing, if you're under the age of 18, you'll want to seek out a parent or guardian who can open a custodial account for you. You'll use any brokerage to open the account; however, the highest and largest ones are Fidelity, Charles Schwab, E*TRADE, and TD Ameritrade (I personally use Fidelity).

Next, you'll want to decide what proportion of money you would like to place in your investment account. I might recommend putting 100% of your savings into the investment account (you don't necessarily have to invest it all) it'll just be available just in case you would like to make a fast trade.

Of the cash you have in the account, I might recommend investing 70–80% of your money due to your minimal day-to-day expenses as an adolescent. One important tip is that the time you opt to open an investment account won't be an equivalent time you'll want to make your first investment. I might recommend following the marketplace for a month or two before you create your first investment that way you begin to find out market behavior and you'll choose your own whether you're buying into your investments at an honest price.

Remember, sometimes the worth you pay is often more important than the past performance of the corporate. After you've bought all of your positions, it's now time to manage your portfolio. I personally wish to check on my investment accounts once a month to ascertain where we're at.

Why It Is Important to Start Investing Early?

So, what is going to take to become a millionaire, say, by retirement? Well, it depends entirely on once you start saving and investing. The sooner you start, the less you have to take a position. If you start investing in the stock exchange at age twenty and mediocre knowledge returns (throughout this book, we'll assume 9.7% annual growth, which is what the broader stock exchange has averaged since the first 1900s), you would like to take a position $173 per month to possess $1 million in your account by age sixty. Not regrettable, right?

If you start investing at eighteen, you'll get to put in just $142 per month to retire a millionaire. And if you start at fifteen, a measly $106 is all that's needed. This is often very doable.

The average American waits until they're thirty-one years old to start saving for retirement which means they're going to invest $522 per month to possess an attempt at retiring a millionaire. Better late than never, I guess? But you see, in my opinion, it's way too late. These people have given up a whole decade of investing help from the world's most powerful force—compounding. Compounding shows that an investment's value is usually far more important than even the quantity of initial money invested.

To envision compounding in my day-to-day life, I prefer to follow what I call the "Cheeseburger Rule."

The Cheeseburger Rule is all about cost. That is, participating in some activity or making a sale now causes me to offer up something else—a lost opportunity. If I plan to leave for dinner with friends and buy a cheeseburger, it costs me around $20 (after the loaded fries and added milkshake, of course). But this cheeseburger has future value because if I instead invested $20 today, what proportion wouldn't it be worth, say, in forty years? Remember that average 9.7% annual return? By foregoing the chance to take a position my $20 at 9.7% for forty years, I'm actually paying $890.23 for this cheeseburger today. By going out with friends now, I'm giving up nearly $900 in the future. Is that the trade I'm willing to make? Maybe, because everyone must eat. However, believe things like this in your lifestyle, and you'll spend money—and save money—differently.

At your age, giving up the newest pair of shoes to, instead, invest money for retirement may be a concept that a lot of you'll struggle to grasp. There's peer pressure all around you encouraging you to spend your money. Well, I'm sure your friends will at some point look great in their new shoes while standing on your yacht! If you would like financial security later in life, this is often the proven method to urge there. Heck—hand your friends this book once you're finished and obtain them to hitch the millionaire mindset themselves!

Similarly, if your money is invested in the stock exchange, it'll experience compounding growth. Your money causes you more money, then that extra cash causes you to get extra money, then that cash makes money, which makes money, which makes extra money, and this goes on and on and on—it is an exponential increase! Now, it's important to notice returns in the stock exchange aren't guaranteed. You'll keep your money in a bank account and earn interest—where the bank pays you to save lots of your money with them to loan it to others—but this interest is never quite 1%. The great thing is that your balance will never go down—unless you spend it. Yes, in a bank account, your money will be compounding, but at a way lower rate. If you invest in the stock exchange, your balance may go down in the short term. Still, the stock exchange has averaged on the brink of 10% annual growth since the first 1900s. There are some years it goes up, and a few years it goes down, but at the end of the day, over time, the stock exchange goes up.

How do Stocks work?

Purchasing stocks make you a part-owner of a company. In this case, you buy ownership of such a firm, but this does not mean that you can join during the executive meetings of the organization. You may vote during meetings if you want to exercise that right.

However, most investors are not concerned about those rights and privileges, but about how to make returns on their investments. This is achieved by selling the stocks of such a company for a profit when it goes up. Also, an investor makes money in stocks if the company is paying dividends. But most stocks don't pay dividends. These are quarterly payments given to shareholders from the funds of a firm.

The IPO—Initial Public Offering is a process whereby companies and organizations issue shares in their stock. After this stage, such shares could be bought and sold among different shareholders and investors alike.

Therefore, you will purchase stock from another shareholder or sell your stock to a potential investor. You cannot buy from the company directly. The stock exchange conducts the trading. Also, each investor or trader needs the services of a stockbroker before buying or selling shares.

Stocks fluctuate in value. It can appreciate or depreciate. Some of the factors that can affect the prices of stocks include market volatility to peculiar events in the company such as product recall and communications crisis. But long-term stock investors benefit more. Such persons purchase stocks through index funds and mutual funds. These portfolios pool various investments together.

Strategies for Investing in Stocks

Use Sector Mutual Funds

Investing in businesses operating in a particular sector of the economy is called sector mutual funds. These are designed as ETFs (Exchange-traded funds) and mutual funds. Be prepared to experience fluctuations in the values of stocks, since these equities are not diversified.

You can invest in sector funds using passive and active fund management processes. Companies belong to different sectors of the economy. Investing in sector mutual funds involves choosing stocks from particular areas of the economy. The firms in a sector produce similar products.

Therefore, we have the agricultural sector, pharmaceutical sector, technology sector, and financial sector. Some sectors can provide investors with high growth potentials if they have viable economic activities. You can diversify sector funds through holdings in various portfolios. All these portfolios came with similar risks.

But firms involved in consumer staple stocks such as household items, food items, beverages, and other similar products are usually stable in different market cycles.

Using Consumer Staples Exchange-Traded Funds

Firms specialized in dealing with essential commodities and services regarded as inelastic products provide consumer staples equities. These stocks are regarded as exchange-traded funds (ETFs). The products traded under this category include tobacco, personal care items, foodstuffs, household products, and beverages.

Examples of consumer staple exchange-traded funds include Invesco DWA Consumer Staples Momentum ETF, First Trust Nasdaq Food and Beverage ETF, IShares Evolved U.S Consumer Staples ETF, etc.

Through I Bonds

One of the most secured investments to make includes I bond. It is a liquid financial tool as it is designed with guarantees and the interest rate is not taxable. I bonds are created to mitigate the effects of inflation through stable interest rates.

This type of investment fund cannot be sold within the first year of its existence. Therefore, most investors use it as a second-tier emergency fund. As you create a larger and longer-term portfolio using I bonds, you need to have other sources of cash to meet your needs. The maximum deposit in I bonds per year is $10,000. Therefore, you can use Treasury through TreasuryDirect to open an account, but the accruable interest is not taxable.

To start this transaction, simply open an account with TreasuryDirect. Then, link your bank account for the purposes of fund transfers. Transfer the required cash for purchasing I bonds.

Use Cash

You can use cash to invest in equities through a cash app called Square's Cash app. It has a feature designed for buying and selling stocks. This form of stock investing is a new way to set up your stock market account and get it funded.

Put Options

Put options are designed to facilitate options trading. The prices of these stocks are dependent on another stock. It provides options to trade for the investor but not the guidelines. The put seller gets a premium for each share to sell the stock to the put buyer.

There are one hundred shares of the basic equity in each contract. However, investors are not required to have the primary stock before selling or buying a put. Purchase a put option if you think that the values of equities will depreciate. But if you feel that the price of the primary stock will remain stable or increase, then write or sell a put option.

EE Savings Bonds

If you are looking for savings products with low-risk features that offer you interest in your investments until the expiration of thirty years, then consider EE savings bonds. You can also convert your savings bond to cash to take care of other projects.

Go to TreasuryDirect and purchase EE bonds online. You may not get it in hard copy again. If you want to redeem your EE bonds or buy and manage them, as the owner of the account, use the web browser on your devices.

Through Motif Investment

You can purchase a low-cost and simple portfolio merged in one package known as Motif investing. It offers you portfolios that have rebalancing features just like Robo-advisors.

Motif investment is a private firm providing an alternative platform for investments just like mutual funds. It also offers the functions of the articulated services of Robo-advisors and exchange-traded funds (ETFs).

With this type of investment, you will get a selection of various investment patterns designed to add value to your portfolio of investments. These motifs include the digital gaming world, social networks, and breakthroughs in biotechnology.

CHAPTER 2:

Trading

Developing the Proper Trading Mindset

Except for a very few fortunate individuals, "get rich quick" schemes never work for anyone. At least legally, thousands of people get lured into dubious schemes such as pyramid-type selling or multilevel marketing because they are told that they can double their investments in a few months. These people often lose money in the end.

So why do these people get enticed into joining these dubious schemes?

- Longing for the freedom that wealth provides
- Greed
- Limited job opportunities

These types of people are easily lured by high-powered selling and hype into believing it's easy to gain wealth by following the program. In so doing, they are led into investing their savings on schemes that are only good on paper. Furthermore, most of these schemes are unsustainable, as proven by simple mathematics.

Stock market trading, however, is a real sound investment if you play it right. It's a business venture that requires guts, common sense, and skill. If you take the time to learn about the tools and rules of this trading form, it can become a lucrative way of earning money. This fact has been proven by people who have made stock trading their primary source of income.

Your goal may be one of the reasons mentioned above but what makes stock trading different from those suspicious schemes is that it is sustainable, and the possible gains you can make are limitless and real.

If these systems really work and never fail, they would have made perfect money-spinners, right? It will be the talk of the town for all traders, and all of them would be using these systems instead of relying on their own trading skills and knowledge. When asked why providers of these systems don't use them for monetary gains themselves, they simply reply that they're sharing the tools for philanthropic reasons.

The system preferred and recommended in this book should not be treated as trading's Holy Grail, but it is more than able to help you by showing whether or not you are "in the money." For you to be successful, you are required to learn all the tools, rules, and skills in this book.

The system offered in this book depends on the specific charting program presented to you and will allow you to see when you should enter a trade and when to leave it with gains intact. You'll learn how to do a safe entry into a trade and exit it during a point in that chart when it is most profitable.

What Is Day Trading?

Day trading is when an investor makes short-term trades that don't last longer than a day. This is done so they can make a profit in a financial market. Some of these individuals are very active as they make several trades in a single day, while other investors can enter the market once and then leave quickly to call it a day. Several investors use the day trading method, and in the current market conditions, day trading is one of the most commonly used strategies by investors. To make money by trading, day traders use financial markets such as commodities, stocks, forex, and cryptocurrency. Since a day trader leaves the market on the same day as they enter it, some people also call it intraday trading. For a day trader, the goal is to profit from the financial changes that occur on the financial security within one day. They are called day traders because, in a normal circumstance, a stock trader in the market only trades during the business days of the week. In comparison, since a day trader has to benefit from intraday trading, they never leave their positions and even operate overnight.

But with all of that said, it is also important to understand that day trading is one of the most misunderstood practices on the stock market. Several scams on the internet involving day trading have lured amateurs into plans which provide no return. Unfortunately, because of these scams, day trading was quickly associated with get-rich-quick scams. Some people in the market still carry on trading cryptocurrency without having sufficient knowledge. Still, there are also several people who have been able to make a fortune because of day trading.

What Makes a Good Day Trader?

A person who has been day trading cryptocurrency for a long time as a hobby or as a career will more or less be established in the field. They have detailed knowledge of the industry and also understand which risks are worth taking. Here are some of the character traits you'll need if you're trying to succeed as a day trader in the cryptocurrency world.

Knowing How to Trade

There are two ways a day trader can trade cryptocurrencies. They can either hope that the currency they own increases in price or buy another crypto in an attempt to exchange. Both of these methods can have their advantages and disadvantages, but a seasoned crypto day trader knows when to use the right one.

They Stick to the Popular Currencies

Even though cryptocurrencies aren't regulated by a governmental body, all of them are different because of varying characteristics. Top-notch currencies like:

- Bitcoin,
- Bitcoin Cash,
- Ethereum,
- Ripple, and
- Monero

They are often ranked as some of the best currencies you can trade. Comparing these currencies to coins that are never looked at by day traders is a mistake! By sticking to popular currencies, a day trader earns big and continues to stay at the top. A good currency is also increasingly volatile, has a higher trading volume, and will move the way you're expecting it to move! Since a day trader relies heavily on intraday movement, it is imperative to trade with currencies that have high demand.

If you're trying to succeed as a crypto day trader, it would be best that you start your journey with the currencies we've listed above! These ensure good movements and will make crypto profitable for you.

When Capital Is Low They Trade Less Valuable Currencies

Out of all the cryptocurrencies, you can trade, bitcoin is the one that requires the highest of margins. If you're low on capital, there's no shame in trading currencies that can't attract high margins! Cryptocurrencies like Litecoin and Ripple have margin costs that are lower than those of Bitcoin.

They Pay Attention to the News

If you're thinking of day trading a cryptocurrency, it's vital you stay on top of the news. The problem here is that while the foreign exchange or stock market can easily provide you with a news calendar, the cryptocurrency world does not have one! You constantly have to stay on top of things by looking for information rigorously.

Because of this reason, a seasoned crypto day trader always has a reliable news source that they can trust. This can be especially useful when a sharp change in a currency's movement can be noticed.

Practicing Day Trading Cryptocurrency

At the time when the value of Bitcoin touched $20,000 every person who knew even a little about trading crypto considered themselves to self-proclaimed experts. Beginners who were jumping on the bandwagon didn't have a lot of sources to rely on, so they considered advice from these experts to be legitimate. But as we know by now, the world of crypto can be ruthless and unpredictable. Unless you don't have actual hands-on experience, understanding what works and what doesn't can be complex.

What Swing Trading?

Before you start swing trading, you should think about a few things. Consider what kind of swing trader you want to be before you go out and buy that fancy laptop or open that brokerage account. The first step is to determine how much time you should spend on swing trading. You could be a full-time trader for a company and consider yourself trading for a living, or you could do it part-time for extra money to become a full-time trader in the future.

Many swing traders work full-time and only have a limited amount of time to trade. As a result, they swing trade mainly to increase the returns on their investment accounts, or they might already be retired and want to use trading to expand their assets over time.

The idea is that you can swing trade whether you work full-time or not, but your strategy will differ based on whether you can watch the market all day. By the way, staying up all night watching the market isn't going to help you make more money. It will decrease your profits if it causes you to overtrade or respond to market gyrations. Here are a few examples of what swing trading can be for you:

Swing Trading as Your Primary Source of Income

Swing traders who work full-time jobs for several hours a day should expect to spend months, if not years, gaining experience until they can leave their job and trade full-time from home. They research potential transactions before, during, and aftermarket hours. They're also robust under duress.

The pressures of full-time trading are too much for many traders. After all, if swing trading is your primary source of income, you're under a lot of pressure to make steady gains, and if you've had a run of losses, you'll be more tempted to gamble. Many traders are unaware that the only way to recover from a string of losses is to do less trading. Take a step back to assess the situation; don't quit your day job because you're making a lot of money for a few months. The goal of this game is to earn enough money to come back and play again.

Swing Trading to Boost Income or Improve Investment Returns

This category encompasses the vast majority of swing traders. Swing trading for fun or to boost the returns on your portfolio is less burdensome than swing trading for a living. You have plenty of options if you make a mistake, and you can swing trade when working full-time.

Part-time work swing traders often perform their research when they get home from work and then execute trades the next day. In addition, if they are unable to track the market continuously, they may use stop-loss orders to protect their money. If you want to swing trade full time in the future, you should pass through this stage first.

Swing trading part-time is ideal for those who have a full-time job and can dedicate a few hours per week to market and security research. If you have a passion for capital markets and short-term trading, as well as the discipline to place stop-loss orders regularly, you should try part-time swing trading. You should fit into the criteria for part-time swing trading if you don't gamble with your own money or are unlikely to double down or take significant risks.

Sneaking a Peek at the Swing Trader's Strategic Plan

Please note these important terms; Plan your trade and exchange your scheme. You don't prepare and plan to fail.

Numerous perceptions highlight the value of a trading plan. The business plan of your business is a trading plan. You would probably fall into the pit of making things happen as you go without the strategy. Your business would be unreasonable, you're not going to change and you're not going to have the trading records. You may assume that your trading strategy is in your mind but it doesn't work for all purposes if you haven't written it down.

Trading Strategies

Day trading is not really a trading strategy, as it only determines that you don't want to leave an open trade overnight. It is instead a trading style. In this Day Trading Options Guide, we will be looking at the most popular day trading strategies for beginners and advanced traders.

Arbitrage Strategy

Arbitrage is, in theory, a situation where an investor can make a profit without any risk. If an investor uses arbitrage as his strategy, he intends to take advantage of market pricing errors. An arbitration situation may arise, for example, when a share of a specific company is valued at a different level in different marketplaces (stock exchanges), in which case, by buying a share from one market, it can be sold at a higher price in another.

An arbitrage situation can also arise between two different products. Arbitrage is considered to play an essential role in keeping the market efficient. Once an arbitrage situation arises, market participants begin to take advantage of it, leading to a price difference and ultimately to the disappearance of the arbitrage itself.

Risk-Free Arbitrage Strategy

The risk-free arbitrage of options is based on the parity formula arbitrage (conversion/anti-conversion arbitrage), supplemented by discount arbitrage, box arbitrage, etc. The principle is mainly to capture the trading opportunities when there is a difference between the options market's trading price and its theoretical value.

In mature overseas markets, due to institutional investors' massive participation and the improvement of the market trading mechanism (mainly reflected in the rise of electronic trading methods and high-frequency traders), the time and space of risk-free arbitrage have significantly been reduced. For instance, Life Statistics from the 2005 options exchange show that the duration of arbitrage opportunities has dropped from an average of 3 minutes in 2001 to within 4 seconds.

Parity Formula Arbitrage

Parity formula arbitrage can be divided into conversion and anti-conversion arbitrage.

The arbitrage strategy's theoretical basis comes from the option parity relationship, that is, the inevitable relationship between the European option and the put option price of the underlying asset.

Among them, C is the call option price (option premium), P is the put option price (option premium), K is the option exercise price, S is the underlying spot price, r is the risk-free interest rate, and T is the remaining term.

This arbitrage strategy is an essential guarantee that the price of call and put options can be maintained at a reasonable level.

Specifically, conversion arbitrage is composed of buying a spot target, buying put options, and selling call options simultaneously, where the exercise price of each option is the same as the expiration date.

Trading Mistakes to Avoid

For most, trading can be challenging, regardless of their experience level. The trading strategy, emotions, and analysis all play an important role when it comes to doing your best.

However, more often than not, a trader will end up making some sort of mistake. No matter your experience level, the following are the five most common mistakes made by traders.

Tops and Bottoms

The interest in grabbing a bottom or top is tempting. There is a large appeal in a contrarian market approach, but unless there is a really good reason, lock in your profits before the top of a top or bottom of a bottom.

The main reason why a trader will chase the tops and bottoms is psychology. Traders think that the market, especially right after a strong trend, will change to enter into a new trend. This can lead a trader into taking a bad position. The fact is that trends can only be validated when the price has moved considerably from its support or resistance level and even the best traders or analysts will find it extremely hard to call a bottom or top. To ensure you do not fall prey to chasing tops and bottoms, you have to set your impulses and emotions aside and look at the market objectively.

Bad Risk Management

The interesting thing is that, for the most part, traders tend to be correct in their analysis. What they tend to get wrong is their money management. Entering a big position quickly because your analysis shows that the prices will probably turn may end up leaving you at risk of the prices continuing to grow.

When you have too much first position exposure, it may become difficult to manage your trade goes wrong. There are two golden rules that every trader should follow:

- Always expect your first position to be wrong and use a smaller first position.
- Increase your position when your first position is proven to be correct.

These two rules will enable you to think critically, lower your losses and increase profits. Review these rules every month to ensure they set into your trading plan.

Allowing Losses to Pile Up

One of the most important characteristics of a successful trader is being able to get out of a position with a small loss quickly if they see a trade is not going to work out and they then move onto the next trade. On the other hand, the unsuccessful trader will become paralyzed if their trade goes against them. Instead of acting quickly to cap their loss, they tend to hold their position in the hopes of the trade working out. In addition to tying up their capital for a long period of time and becoming a bag holder, this type of inaction could cause mounting losses and depletion of their capital.

Failure to Make Use of Stop-Loss Orders

This is a mistake linked to the one above. To be successful in trading, you have to have use stop-loss orders. The failure to implement this one is the worst mistake that you can make. A tight stop-loss typically means that a loss will be capped before they become too large. A 10% stop-loss below your buy price is usually sensible. So if you invest $100 you can only lose a maximum of $10 returning you majority of your capital.

Not Sticking to or Not Creating a Trading Plan

Experienced traders always need to have a trading plan. The plan will help traders know when they will enter and exit, how much they will invest, and the max loss they will take. A novice trader may end up not having a plan before they start trading. Even if they have come up with a plan, they are more likely to abandon it than the more experienced traders if they think things are not going to plan.

CHAPTER 3:

Bitcoin

Investing in Bitcoin

Over the past few years, there have been a number of complaints about Bitcoin. The original Bitcoin was developed with only 21 million coins available. These coins would slowly be added to the market as miners completed their codes to keep the chains of the blockchain secure. Many people worry that this amount of coins will not be enough, especially when considering how many people throughout the world are starting to use these digital currencies. There are also some issues with the speed of Bitcoin. Bitcoin Cash is meant to be an alternative to Bitcoin and is meant to help solve some of the problems that we talked about before. It is easy to get started with Bitcoin Cash.

You can either start out right away with Bitcoin Cash. Or, if you already have Bitcoin, you are allowed to switch these out for Bitcoin Cash and start using these if you would like.

Investing in Cryptocurrencies

Investing in cryptocurrencies is a fairly easy process. It is not as stringently regulated like the stock market or even the Forex market. That lack of regulation gives it an air of the old west, and this is where you make your money without the intrusion and interference of burgeoning regulation.

While Bitcoin and Ethereum are considered some of the biggest digital currencies that you can invest in right now, there are a lot of other choices that you can go with. Choosing one of these other digital currencies can make a big difference in how much you can make. For example, Bitcoin has been around for some time and has a really high value right now. But going with another option, like one of the options below, can make it easier to get into the market because the current value is much lower.

Let's take a look at some of the other major digital currencies that you can invest in and how to get started with them.

Investing in Litecoin

You can also choose to invest in Litecoin. In fact, this is one of the options that are available through the popular exchange site known as Coinbase. Litecoin is a peer-to-peer currency that will enable you to send instant, low-cost payments, to anyone you would like to throughout the world. It is completely decentralized and opens sourced, making it similar to Bitcoin in these ways. It is one of the top digital currencies, following Ethereum and Bitcoin and often tied with Ripple.

So, how is Litecoin different from Bitcoin and some of the other digital currencies? First, Litecoin is going to work with a software algorithm to mine units. This can help prevent individuals from making customer computers to mine the currency. In addition, the transaction times with Litecoin are one of the fastest of all the currencies. Right now, Litecoin can get transactions done in less than three minutes, while it usually takes Bitcoin about ten minutes.

Investing in Dash

Some people choose to work with a currency known as Dash. This is a cryptocurrency that has made it its mission to solve some of the problems that have come up with Bitcoin. It is known as an open-source cryptocurrency that split off from Litecoin in 2014. This currency is mainly working on solving the issue of speed that is found in Bitcoin. With Bitcoin, it can take minutes to resolve a transaction, something that isn't going to work in a world where things need to be done instantly.

The biggest problem is that purchasing Dash is not going to be the easiest, which can slow down how fast it becomes popular. To purchase the coins, you will first need to go to Coinbase and purchase some Bitcoin. You can then use your Bitcoin to go to Bitsane and purchase the Dash that you want to use. Until that issue is solved, it may be hard for Dash to take off. There are rumors that Coinbase may be adding Dash to their network, but that has not happened yet.

Investing in Dogecoin

Dogecoin is a digital currency that is similar to Bitcoin. It was introduced in December of 2013. This currency has made it through bearish and bullish markets and is often seen as a tipping currency. What this means is that you can tip someone with Dogecoin rather than using upvotes and likes on social media.

Right now, Dogecoin is not worth all that much, but this can make it a good one to invest in because the price will be so low to join. How this market works is that when you are on a certain website or a social media page, you can tip the other person for the hard work that they do. It is not going to provide them with a lot of money, but as a tip, and if a lot of people tip at the same time, the owner could make some money.

Investing in Ripple

Another popular digital currency that you can work with is known as Ripple. Ripple is known as a settlement network that is used to transfer any currency to someone no matter where they are located in the world. Rather than having to use systems like the Western Union or SWIFT and waiting for days to get the money to the right place (and dealing with high fees in the process), you can get the transaction done within a few seconds.

Right now, Ripple focuses its attention on working with banks. This works well because Ripple offers a cost-effective and efficient way for customers to send payments all around the world.

Buy and Sell Cryptocurrency

Trading cryptocurrencies are all about a repeated process of buying and selling. However, you cannot just buy and sell cryptocurrencies at random. Each buys and sell order that you make should be made strategically and backed up with solid research. When buying and selling a cryptocurrency, it is important to note that there is a difference between the buy price and the selling price.

You will be glad to hear that purchasing these digital currencies is not difficult. But, you do need to have a good idea of what you are looking for. If you want to go with one of the more popular digital currencies, then the best exchange site to work with is Coinbase. Coinbase will allow investors to exchange Litecoin, Ethereum, and Bitcoin.

There are many sites you can buy crypto, some of them includes:

- Binance
- Bittrex
- Conbase
- Cashapp
- Coin exchange
- Jubiter.com

The buying price is always higher than the selling price. This is mainly how a broker earns a profit. Before you buy and sell any cryptocurrency be sure to do research to see the prevailing market rate for buying and selling.

A good way to do this is by viewing the rates offered by different reputable brokers. You should also check the price of the cryptocurrency that you want to buy/sell on coinmarketcap and coingecko just to give you an idea of the prevailing rate. You may find some slight differences in the price also considering that the prices of the different cryptocurrencies in the market continuously fluctuate. Always remember the number one trading principle: Buy low, sell high.

Selling is just as important as buying. Selling is where you finally close your position and turn your cryptocurrency into fiat money. Reputable cryptocurrency wallets like Coinbase will allow you to sell cryptocurrencies directly from your Coinbase wallet. If your wallet does not allow you to sell cryptocurrencies, then you should open a trading account with a trustworthy broker.

Contrary to want other people think, selling cryptocurrency also takes skill and strategy. It is not just about converting a cryptocurrency into cash, but it is also about proper timing. Any of these three things that can happen when you sell a cryptocurrency:

- You are in a profit already, and you would like to sell your cryptocurrency to finally close your position and turn your profit into cash, or;
- You accepted your losses and would like to sell your cryptocurrency to avoid possible future losses, or;
- You sell your cryptocurrency only to regret it when the price increases after selling your cryptocurrency.

Of course, there is also the lingering idea of not selling your cryptocurrency and hoping that its price will continuously increase. However, when you take this approach, you should also consider the risk that the price of the cryptocurrency concerned might suddenly drop. Again, do not underestimate the high volatility of the cryptocurrency market. As you can see, selling a cryptocurrency can also be quite complicated. There are things that you should consider. Before you sell your cryptocurrency, it is advised that you should first study the cryptocurrency market. The more that you understand the cryptocurrency market, especially the cryptocurrency that you intend to buy/sell, the more like that you can come up with the right trading decision. Keep in mind that you are dealing with a constantly moving and evolving market. You cannot just buy and sell cryptocurrencies at random. You must have the right understanding and apply an effective strategy to significantly increase your chances of making a profitable trade.

Purchase Risk

There is a risk that you face when you purchase coins from unknown sellers. Especially if you are doing it with fiats. There is a chance that once you pay for it, they do not transfer the coin. So that is a risk that you must contend with when you find a broker to purchase the coin and when you start trading. There are two strategies to overcome this. The first is that you can buy the coin from a reputable seller. That way you deposit the funds and the coins are certain to reach your wallet. From there you transfer the contents of your wallet to a hosted wallet with the trading broker. Then you can make whatever trades you want. That takes out the purchase risk. But you still have one more risk when it comes to trading.

What most people do not understand is that there are a number of trading houses out there that operate on the fringe. What they do is take your coin (be it BTC, Ethereum, or Monero) and they then make the purchase on the market or you. Sometimes, they do not make the actual purchase and they just record the ledger as the purchase being made. This happens a lot in all brokerages because one of the ways traditional financial brokers work is that they buy popular assets in bulk, keep some for themselves and their discretionary accounts, then apportion the rest out to other customers who also bought them.

CHAPTER 4:

Bitcoin Trading

What Is Cryptocurrency?

To understand what cryptocurrency is, you have to first decipher the meaning of the term.

Cryptography is the science of transmitting data in a way where only people authorized to see the data, can see it and understand it. Thus, cryptocurrency is any digital currency that uses cryptography for protection. Because of this enhanced security feature, it is impossible to create a counterfeit. In addition, the originator of cryptocurrency can control its production. This means that all the time, demand will always outweigh the supply, thus making cryptocurrency very popular. It also means that cryptocurrency cannot be controlled or manipulated by governments. It is devoid of interference by nature. These benefits make cryptocurrency more attractive day by day.

In 2009, a pseudonymous entity known by the name Satoshi Nakamoto launched the first-ever cryptocurrency in the world of computers—Bitcoin. Barely six years later, there were about 14 million BTC coins in the world worth an estimated $3.4 billion. Quite huge! This great value contributed to the extreme growth of Bitcoin, much more than other digital currencies.

Since 2009, we can say that this secret money market has never looked back. It has continued to get better, with more people looking for digital currency.

It has increased more than a hundredfold in value. As more and more people come to trust and use cryptocurrencies, the value has only increased, making the holders of these currencies richer.

You could be one of them if you are brave enough to believe and trust the technology. With large financial institutions like JP Morgan Chase seeing the potential in Bitcoin and other cryptocurrencies, because of their cheap transaction costs, the currencies can only get better.

The cost for the transfer of funds and other payments is very cheap—way cheaper than what banks charge. Another quality is safety. Although there have been some thefts in the future with some Bitcoin lost, it is much safer than most other currencies we have in the world. Since it exists purely in digital form, it is much safer than other currencies, and transactions can be done super-fast. We will be looking at the safety of Bitcoin later, in more detail.

Should you get on the bandwagon today then? If you have not already, you should! The money train just went digital. While paper, coin, and plastic currency are not going anywhere soon, we can say the future is here with cryptocurrency.

The Most Common Types of Cryptocurrencies

Unlike what many beginners think, there are more cryptocurrencies than just Bitcoin, and more will come up in the future. However, you are smart if you only know of Bitcoin, because it is way ahead of the pack. It is most popular; it started this wonderful technological revolution. So, Bitcoin it is! A name for the other cryptocurrencies has been coined and they are collectively referred to as altcoins or alternative coins.

Without any centralized authority over Bitcoin, we can say that it has practically set the trends for most other cryptocurrencies in the market. The other coins are the enhanced versions of Bitcoin; but the truth is that if Bitcoin was not here, they too would not be here.

Today, there are more than 1,000 cryptocurrencies. In the future, this number can only go up. However, Bitcoin will remain way ahead of the pack, being the most preferred coin in the world since it is backed by perfect technology.

With so many cryptocurrencies in the market, what others are worth your attention? Well, take your pick from the few presented below:

Ethereum

The value of Ethereum as of June 2020 was $ 244.66.

In your search for information online, you will find Ethereum mentioned in many circles. This is another type of digital money, decentralized, and made to run without any form of interference, control, or fraud.

However, the most interesting part of it is the Ether, a cryptographic token that is used by developers to codify, secure, and run applications (other than money) on the Ethereum platform.

It occupies second place after Bitcoin in terms of value and distribution. Over time, Ethereum has become the technology of choice for many people, as it can be used to encrypt, codify, trade, and do much more in a very decentralized manner.

Only a few years of being in the market since it was released in 2015, Ethereum is worth looking into if you would like to diversify your cryptocurrency portfolio.

Litecoin

The value of Litecoin as of June 2020 was $ 46.58.

Called LTC, Litecoin has been present a good number of years in the market, and it is regarded second only to Bitcoin. It is perfect for you if you would like to diversify your coin portfolio.

It is built on the same concept as Bitcoin, i.e. decentralized, peer-to-peer computer networking, storage, and backup; most importantly, it uses a technology called scrypt for security.

This technology can be decoded by consumer-grade CPUs, thus making it possible for everyone to invest in Litecoin.

There are caps designed to keep Litecoin safe from inflation. For example, it is said that the value of Litecoin in the market cannot exceed $84 million. This is designed to keep it scarce, attractive, and valuable for a good number of years.

Who uses Litecoin? Like Bitcoin, the list of international merchants who accept Litecoin continues to grow. Apart from that, developers and software vendors have no qualms at all about being paid in LTC.

BitcoinCash

The value BitcoinCash as of June 2020 was $ 254.92.

While this is not exactly Bitcoin despite the relationship in names, it is a nice investment avenue that is up and coming very quickly. It is largely used by Bitcoin enthusiasts, but it is not expected to rise too high.

Dogecoin

The value as of June 2020 was $0.00258232.

Would you believe this coin was created just for fun, and when it was released, it was found it had staying power? It is not supposed to do as well as Litecoin, but it is in many features, similar to Litecoin. If you are a true Cryptocurrency enthusiast, maybe you can add several Dogecoins to your portfolio.

Namecoin

The value as of June 2020 was $0.486094.

This is regarded the same as Bitcoin because initially it was designed to be an upgrade of Bitcoin; later on, it seemed much better to release it as a standalone coin, fearing that it could cause problems if released as an upgrade. While it is a direct spinoff of Bitcoin, it is still very low in value.

Ripple

The value as of June 2020 was $0.203532.

Although it is one of the cheapest cryptocurrencies in the market, Ripple has been integrated into some banks, thanks to its design and purpose. It was created in 2012 as a remittance network, for currency exchange and gross settlement. With that kind of progress and purpose in the market, this coin will stick around even though it is one of the cheapest in the market today.

SexCoin

As of June 2020, the price for SexCoin was $0.00213763.

What a name for cryptocurrency and yes, this coin was created to help you stay anonymous if you are a consumer of adult content on the web. Thus, instead of using your credit card or bank wire for paying for such services, you can use SexCoin.

CHAPTER 5:

The Future of Cryptocurrency

The Future of Cryptocurrency

Many cryptocurrencies saw a lot of growth in recent years, with some like Bitcoin, Bitcoin Cash, Dash, and Ethereum seeing exponential growth. As we move forward, the cryptocurrency space will only keep growing. According to some industry experts, the coming year will see mass public awareness for cryptocurrencies. Here are some of the things expected to happen in the cryptocurrency world in the future:

Taxation Will Become a Huge Issue

While many people have amassed wealth in the cryptocurrency market, many have been keeping it away from the eyes of the government. In the coming years, you can expect that the IRS will be more focused on clamping down on cryptocurrency investors, to make sure they pay their taxes.

Bitcoin to Develop into a Payment Network

Though it was meant to be an electronic payments system, many people currently consider Bitcoin as a store of value and a speculative asset. However, according to Trevor Konerko, CEO of a cryptocurrency technology company, Bitcoin's utility and price will increase dramatically, leading to its emergence as a fully-fledged payment network. This will be driven by the emergence of scaling solutions such as Lightning Network. However, for Bitcoin to become a fully-fledged payment network, its community needs to be willing to adopt these upgrades.

Cryptocurrencies Are Here to Stay

To some people, cryptocurrencies are a passing fad, something that will lose momentum as fast as it gained it. However, industry experts believe that cryptocurrencies and blockchain technology are here to stay. Some platforms like NEO and Ethereum will push for the widespread adoption of the technology since they help people create blockchain applications that have meaningful uses in the real world. The adoption of these real-world applications by the corporate world will increase the demand for cryptocurrencies and will therefore ensure their longevity.

Diversification of Assets by Investors

Currently, most investors hold their assets in Bitcoin and Ethereum. However, you can expect that more people will start diversifying their portfolios into other cryptocurrencies like Dash, Litecoin, IOTA, NEM, and many more. Many investors will diversify their cryptocurrency assets, in the same way, that they approach other traditional assets. Many more cryptocurrencies will also emerge in the coming years. Some will be introduced, tackle the challenges being experienced by existing cryptocurrencies, while others will introduce new niches altogether. There is a high likelihood that some of the new cryptocurrencies will become very profitable.

Increased Regulation

Currently, many countries do not have any policies for cryptocurrencies. However, several governments have been keenly watching their use and growth. As more people adopt cryptocurrencies, governments will start putting regulations in place surrounding their use.

Cryptocurrencies Will Force Conventional Financial Systems to Level Up

Currently, banks and traditional payment processors are enjoying extremely high transaction fees. They are also very slow, with most international transactions being processed in 1–3 days. Cryptocurrencies, on the other hand, are very fast and have extremely low processing fees. These advantages might push more businesses towards cryptocurrencies. If they are to remain relevant, banks and traditional payment processors will need to up their game.

Technological Future

Cryptocurrency, as a concept, has a bright technological future. Increasingly powerful computers accompanied by an algorithm that is becoming easier to mine means that cryptocurrency will be less cumbersome to mine.

Changing Dominance

Currently, Bitcoin is the leading cryptocurrency. However, as technology advances and as demand for tokens increases, there will be a shift towards other cryptocurrencies. Thus, Bitcoin is likely to cede ground in the future as the dominant cryptocurrency. Nonetheless, its position as the "gold" standard of cryptocurrencies is going to remain unchallenged for a long time. Ripple, Litecoin, and Ethereum are going to take a greater role in the near future, as many financial institutions are actively exploring them. Ripple is being preferred to form an automated algorithmic clearinghouse. Ethereum is attractive due to its many customizable features such as smart contracts, among others.

Performance of Fiat Currency

One of the main factors that have driven many people towards cryptocurrency, is the instability of their own fiat currencies. For example, Zimbabwean Dollar has become worthless. The Venezuelan Bolivar has depreciated at such a high rate that it is hard to keep it as a store of value.

When a given fiat currency becomes unstable, users become more willing to take up cryptocurrency. In most jurisdictions where the economy is overheating, to such an extent that they are facing hyperinflation, countries restrict the flow of foreign currency so that people cannot buy them. Since governments have no control over cryptocurrencies, they can become the available options for citizens to safeguard their monetary investment.

How to Invest in Cryptocurrencies?

Investment is about safeguarding your earnings or wealth into programs that not only enable them to be secure but also grow in value.

For an investment to be deemed as a promising investment, it must have:

- A standard of measure
- A store of value
- Converted into a form that is universally recognized as an investment option

Cryptocurrencies such as Bitcoin differ from fiat currencies (government-issued currencies) due to their limited volume. This means that when someone hoards a unit, fewer units are available for circulation into the market. For example, Bitcoin has a maximum volume of 21 million tokens. Litecoin has a maximum volume of 84 million tokens. This is unlike fiat currency where that unit could be replaced by the printing of more units.

Due to the limited supply of cryptocurrencies, hoarding and speculation have become the norm. Hoarding acts as a means of investing in cryptocurrency. Speculation becomes the real driver that determines whether one should hoard or release his/her hoarded stock to the market.

Establish a Measure of Your Investment

Every investment has a yardstick for measuring its value. When it comes to fiat currencies, US Dollar remains the international yardstick. When it comes to commodity currencies, gold remains the yardstick. Cryptocurrencies also have their yardstick—Bitcoin.

Bitcoin—the "gold" standard of cryptocurrency.

Bitcoin is the first cryptocurrency to use blockchain technology. Prior to Bitcoin, there had been many unsuccessful attempts. Bitcoin became the first successful attempt. Bitcoin has dominated the cryptocurrency market such that it has become the de facto cryptocurrency standard just as gold remains the de facto standard for both commodity and fiat currency.

Its dominant position and recognition as a cryptocurrency standard have made other cryptocurrencies to be termed "altcoins," which simply means "alternative coins/cryptocurrencies."

Thus, to be able to establish the performance of your investment in the cryptocurrency market, you have to gauge it against Bitcoin.

What are the failures of fiat currency that cryptocurrency has come to remedy?

While you desire to invest in cryptocurrency, you need to understand its rationale. Why does it exist? What problem(s) was it created to solve?

From an investment perspective, the following are some of the failures of fiat currency that cryptocurrency has come to remedy:

- Low returns
- Low levels of speculation
- Unlimited supply
- Government manipulation
- **Legal limitations**—sanctions, political upheavals, etc.

The Best Cryptocurrency to Invest in

Which is the best cryptocurrency for investors? Many would-be investors ponder this question before making an investment decision. However, unlike investment in securities and forex, cryptocurrency is a relatively new phenomenon. It is not easy to predict which cryptocurrencies will last and which ones will eventually collapse.

You can easily choose a currency to trade in but, investment, being long-term, is not such an easy choice. The best thing to do is to follow the old adage "never put all your eggs in one basket." Every investor knows the importance of diversification when it comes to dealing with highly risky and volatile markets. The cryptocurrency market is extremely risky and volatile. It is not a market for the risk-averse. It is a market for risk-takers.

Why go for high-risk volatile markets such as cryptocurrency? The underlying principle of investment is "high risk, high returns." In simple terms, the higher the risk, the higher is the potential for higher returns. You never get much return on a risk-proof investment.

While Bitcoin has shown high potential, this does not guarantee that it will never fade into obscurity. New blockchain and non-blockchain technologies are emerging. Many cryptocurrencies have already submerged into obscurity while more are coming up. You cannot ignore Bitcoin, but you have to look beyond Bitcoin as you diversify your portfolio.

How to Buy Cryptocurrency?

Acquiring a cryptocurrency is the first step to owning it. While miners can acquire cryptocurrencies without buying them, you as an investor will have to buy them. Once you decide on your portfolio and the cryptocurrencies to buy based on your portfolio, you will have to look out for a trading platform where you can buy your cryptocurrencies. We shall look at these cryptocurrency trading platforms in our next section. While there are many cryptocurrencies, not all of them are traded on every platform. The only cryptocurrencies that you can easily find on most platforms are:

- Bitcoin
- Ethereum
- Litecoin

For the other cryptocurrencies, you have to ascertain the platform that it is traded.

How to Store Cryptocurrency for a Long-Term Hold?

Cold storage is a term that refers to the storage of cryptocurrencies for the long-term hold. Due to their digital or virtual nature, you need to store your coins on a medium that will not allow your digital codes/keys to be erased, either due to blackout, virus attack, or other forms of attack. An online wallet or your exchange platform is a warm storage facility. They are temporary in nature. They are ideal for traders but not investors. You cannot store them for a long time. Online wallets and exchange platforms can be hacked or even fold up. Cold storage facilities are offline facilities for storing cryptocurrency. The following are some of the common cold storage facilities:

PC Wallet

This is a wallet (folder) that you create on your own personal computer (PC) to store your cryptocurrency codes.

Hardware Wallet

A hardware wallet is a dongle specifically created to store encrypted data. Thus, you can block any other unintended use of your hardware wallet.

Ledger Wallets

These are special kinds of hardware wallets. Unlike dongles, they have their own tiny screens that enable one to monitor and manipulate the storage facility. However, ledger wallets are specifically designed to store certain kinds of cryptocurrencies. Thus, while buying one, you must confirm it can store your kind of cryptocurrency.

Paper Wallets

These are impressions specifically created by software and imprinted onto a paper. To help minimize the risk of erasure, tear and wear, you need to ensure that you have a quality paper. The paper wallets have a QR Code printed on them to help you easily capture the keys into the computer during the transaction.

Brain Wallets

These are biological wallets that you etch into your own memory through the process of coding and consolidation in such a manner that you can easily retrieve the details. The use of mnemonics is the commonest way of creating brain wallets.

Cryptocurrency Investing Strategies

Cryptocurrencies, just like investing in other currencies and investments in securities, require sound investment strategies. While each investor is unique and thus will come up with their own investing strategy, there are still general investing strategies considered by most investors.

The following are the four main investing strategies:

- Unbalanced Portfolio
- Balanced Portfolio
- Profit reinvesting
- Dollar-cost averaging

Unbalanced Portfolio

This is a strategy whereby you allocate every investment depending on your projection of its performance.

For example, if you think Bitcoin will perform the best over time, you would give a significant proportion of investment to it and continue allocating to the next-best downwards based on predetermined percentages:

- Bitcoin (50%)
- XRP (30%)
- Monero (15%)
- DASH (5%)

This strategy is ideal for those investors who are able to carry out extensive research so that they can make informed predictions.

Balanced Portfolio

A balanced portfolio is whereby you allocate all your shortlisted currencies equal share of your portfolio.

For example, if you have a total portfolio fund of $4,000, you will allocate to your best four currencies as follows:

- Bitcoin ($1,000)
- XRP ($1,000)
- Monero ($1,000)
- DASH ($1,000)

Any subsequent investment fund will be allocated equally to your preferred currencies.

This strategy is ideal for those who are not active followers of the currency market and they cannot make more accurate predictions of which of the preferred currencies will perform better than the other.

Profit Reinvesting

Profit Reinvesting is a strategy where you reinvest profits gotten from a profitable portfolio to new currencies to expand the portfolio. This way, profits cover the risk of a new adventure rather than a new source of capital from your pocket. However, you only need to reinvest a given percentage of your profits (e.g. between 10% and 50%).

Reinvesting is a good strategy for long-term investors who are risk-averse yet they are not in a hurry to withdraw their profits.

Dollar-Cost Averaging

Dollar-Cost Averaging is a strategy that allows you to invest a fixed amount of dollars (or any other fiat currency) into cryptocurrency at predetermined intervals. It is more of a blind investment strategy whereby you continue investing to increase your stock level regardless of price movements in the market (for so long as your allocation is enough to buy some currencies). This strategy is ideal for passive investors who do not have time to follow up on market activities on a day-to-day basis. They only need to have a long-term projection of a given currency based on its fundamental analysis to make their investment decision.

The Advantages of Long-term Crypto Investment

Long-term investment in cryptocurrency is about taking a long-term view of a given cryptocurrency in terms of future projections and deciding to commit your resources to it for a longer period.

Less Risk

Short-term investment is prone to short-term swings. Without proper timing, you may lose your short-term investment simply because you waited longer than deserved to recoup your gains. The challenge is that this timing is undefined. You can only estimate it. With a long-term investment, you do not have to be weighed down by the urgency to withdraw your investment to meet other obligations. Thus, when the price is not favorable, you can still wait. Furthermore, with long-term investment, you are focused on the fundamental value of the currency rather than the market forces. The price is low does not necessarily mean that the fundamental value of the currency has gone down. It simply means that the demand is lower than the supply.

Lower Fees

Short-term investment means that you have to keep on withdrawing and re-investing. Both withdrawals and re-investments have their own transaction costs. The more frequently you do it, the higher the transaction cost. On the other hand, long-term investment has a much lower frequency and thus lower transaction cost.

Indicators of Long-term Value

One of the most important things to a long-term investor is the long-term value of a given investment. While you cannot establish with certainty the long-term value of a given cryptocurrency investment, the following are key indicators to watch out for:

Market Share

Market share refers to the percentage of market capitalization that a given currency has relative to the rest of the market. If this market share becomes persistent in its trend, then, that is a solid currency. You can make a long-term investment depending on whether you just want to secure your investment away from other more volatile investments (in case of a horizontal trend) or you want to have long-term gain (in case of an upward trend). Currently, Bitcoins control above 50% of the market share.

Utility

Utility is the ability of a currency to satisfy the market's wants. Currencies that satisfy most consumer's wants (e.g. exchange of value, or store of value) will receive more of their attention and demand than other currencies in the market. A currency with a higher utility in the market will be the most sought-after. It has long-term growth potential (unless it becomes disrupted by a newer currency with a much higher utility). This utility may not be the same for everyone. For example, while individuals may more likely prefer investing in Bitcoins due to their higher utility, financial institutions may prefer investing in Ethereum due to its utility in enabling them to create various forms of smart contracts.

Transaction Volume

Transaction volumes indicate the level of activity of a given currency. A currency that is increasing in its traded volume means it getting more usage while one that is getting declining traded volumes shows that its use is going down.

A currency with a high and increasing transaction volume has a higher long-term value.

Technological Development

Cryptocurrencies have no other value except that derived from their unique technology. Technologically advanced cryptocurrency makes it become increasingly adopted, become the leader of other cryptocurrencies, and the standard benchmark. Thus, a cryptocurrency that keeps on churning new technological breakthroughs (in terms of mining, transacting, and storage) means that it has a long-term future value.

Market Sentiments

Market sentiments can shape the demand for a given currency and thus affect its transaction volume and market share. This can be either positive or negative depending on the market sentiments. Consistently positive market sentiments grant a given cryptocurrency long-term positive value. On the contrary, persistently negative sentiments in the market erode a cryptocurrency's long-term future value.

Risk Appetite as an Influencing Factor of Your Investment Strategy

Risk is an important component of any investment one makes. Equity markets and money markets are, by their very volatile nature, more prone to risk than other investments. Whether you will invest in the long-term or short-term and whether you will choose a riskier, yet higher premium investment or a less risky with lower premium investment depends on your risk appetite.

Your risk appetite will determine whether you are risk-averse (most likely to avoid investing in cryptocurrencies), risk-neutral (most likely to invest in low-risk, low-premium cryptocurrencies in the long term), or risk-seeking (more likely to invest in high-risk, high-premium cryptocurrencies in the short-term).

Risk-averse investors are more likely to invest a smaller proportion of their capital into cryptocurrencies and diversify them widely. Risk-neutral investors are more likely to invest relatively average capital into cryptocurrencies and diversity their modesty. Risk-seekers are more likely to invest a more than average share of their capital into cryptocurrencies and diversify only to a few high-premium currencies (about 2 to 3 high-premium cryptocurrencies).

Starting to Trade Cryptocurrency

Cryptocurrencies are traded differently since they use many different algorithms.

What you need to consider before buying or investing are:

Retailer Acceptance

Owning a cryptocurrency is not any good if you cannot buy things with it. Before you decide to invest, you need to know who will and will not accept it. Some coins are built for certain purposes and were not designed to purchase goods. Some cryptocurrencies are accepted, while others can just be exchanged for other digital coins.

Verification Method

The biggest difference between cryptocurrencies and other currencies is the way they verify transactions. The most common and oldest way is the proof-of-work method. A computer spends energy and time-solving math problems to verify transactions. The problem with this is the computer uses massive amounts of energy just to operate. Systems that use proof-of-stake methods get rid of this problem, by allowing the users who have the biggest share to verify the transactions. This has a faster speed and uses less power to operate. Security concerns mean that fewer coins rely totally on proof-of-stake systems.

Trading Via Coinbase

Let us look at the process of starting to trade cryptocurrencies through Coinbase. It is a fairly simple process, but there are some crucial things you need to understand.

First, you will have to create an account with Coinbase.com, so that you can make a digital currency wallet where you are able to store your digital currency securely.

Connect your Coinbase account with your credit card, bank account, or debit card, so that you will be able to exchange digital currency with your local currency.

You will then trade US dollars for a cryptocurrency of your choice, which will likely be Litecoin or Ethereum, or both.

You should also use a bank account and avoid using a credit/debit card, as bank account fees are a lot lower than credit/debit card fees.

You will have to give them your bank account login when you sign up. It may seem shady, but it is safe and part of the process. You will also have to wait about three to five days to get your bank account approved. You will also have a limit on the amount that you can buy and sell in a single week. When you add a photo ID and other types of payment methods, it will help to increase your limits.

Developing a Trading Algorithm

For any work to be structured and, therefore, successful, we must develop a clear algorithm of actions. Trading is no exception. For example, we cannot start cryptocurrency trading without registering on the exchange or learning how to work with the Tradingview platform. Everything should be done in due order.

Of course, every trader has their own unique path and tailored algorithm of actions. However, as time passes and we gain experience, the sequence of your actions in trading can change. However, we should always have a certain algorithm. This will help save time and avoid financial losses.

Hence, if you need a basic and a short algorithm to start trading, you are welcome. Take a pen and write it down. This algorithm is shallow, but you still can use it and adjust it to your needs and preferences. And now, let us look at this algorithm with a fine-tooth comb and analyze the early stages of your trading in detail.

Reviewing the Cryptocurrency Market Dynamics

The first thing every self-respecting trader should do before they start to trade is analyzed the current situation of the world financial markets. Try to identify the most prevalent activities.

After you find the answers to these questions, determine which coins, based on the information previously received, could be profitable now.

Choosing the Coins

The determining factors in the process of choosing a coin should be its volatility and liquidity.

Volatility is a statistical financial indicator that characterizes the change of a price. It is a crucial indicator in the management of financial risks.

Exploring the Chosen Tools for Trading—Technical and Fundamental Analyses

Technical and fundamental analyses are the main methods of evaluating the market as a whole, and types of cryptocurrency in particular.

Fundamental analysis helps us to determine the general trends and situations in the market, while technical analysis helps to choose the best moments for opening and closing a position.

When put differently, fundamental analysis is a telescope, which allows one to see the whole picture, while technical analysis is a microscope that helps to understand the smallest details.

Following the Latest News

First of all, pay attention to the latest information about the main macroeconomic indicators and news about particular coins. Macro statistics affect the volatility of financial instruments and the activity of traders around the world.

To stay informed, I strongly recommend that you remember, or even better, write down the exact time and day of the week when a news report on a particular coin is released. To simplify news monitoring, I recommend creating a separate tab (page) of a calendar of statistics on your computer, and to view it from time to time.

Drawing Up a Trading Plan

Although this section seems very simple, it is actually quite complicated, as it is the most important part of the activities of any trader.

If you think that you can open a position, after just scrolling through the newsfeed about a particular coin and making a technical analysis of its chart, you need to reconsider that.

Of course, you may be lucky once, but in the long term, this method will result in permanent losses. A trading plan is a prearranged, detailed scenario of a trader's actions in various market situations. That is before you open a position, you determine the possible movements in a coin's price and the reaction of the bulk of traders. At the same time, we should not forget about the time when the news about a certain coin release. Thus, having viewed the calendar of events and understood which time the statistics are released, you get the time of the highest volatility. This time is best suited to the most risk-loving and morally sound traders. Therefore, I do not recommend sluggish traders being active, fifteen minutes before or after the news about a coin release.

Understanding the Psychology of Trading Participants

Although many traders miss this step, I view it as one of the most important prerequisites for successful trading. After all, psychology, namely the sense of the market and a traded coin as well as an understanding of the desires of traders at a given time, are the lion's share of your profitable trades. In my opinion, about 70% of success comes from psychology; 20% from the systems of risk management and money management; and only 10% from your trading strategy. Therefore, once again, review your attitude towards the importance of understanding market participants' psychology.

Looking for Entry Points, Planning Stop Loss, and Take Profit Placement

The fourth and fifth steps of our algorithm can brief you on an entry point. However, one should not treat the choice of such an important aspect too superficially. First, let us determine what the entry point is.

You should be very responsible when choosing the entry point, as the first step in trading has an impact on the final result and its size.

A stop-loss order is an order regarding the price level of an instrument on the chart, by which you close your position at a loss. In other words, you set the sum you are willing to risk in case of a price reversal.

Watch Out for When Trading Cryptocurrency

Whether you look at cryptocurrency as just an alternative transactional mode, or as the next big thing in investment, you ought to be aware of the potential dangers of this new currency on the block.

Absence of Government Regulation

In the case of cryptocurrency, there is not a single international government that has established a comprehensive framework for the regulation and monitoring of transactions denominated by cryptocurrency. Some governments have let organizations and individual users decide for themselves, while other governments have taken the extreme route of outright banning transactions in cryptocurrency. The perils of investing in any cryptocurrency, in such a de-regulated climate, cannot be ignored.

Remember to Wait Until the Transaction Is Approved

Cryptocurrency relies on the approval of a transaction, to ensure that the money is really transferred. Therefore, if you are a seller, never act too hastily when a cryptocurrency transaction is complete. Always wait for approval no matter how much time it takes. The approval comes from the systems that are keeping track of all the transactions; therefore, it might take some time.

Decentralization

Remember that cryptocurrency is a much-decentralized type of currency. There are no banks that have a hold of it, and it does not emanate from a single location. The currency depends on the thousands of people, who keep their systems running all the time, by keeping a track of the transactions that are carried out.

If you fall into any sort of trouble, you might choose to go to a number of places for help; but none of them may be able to offer you a solution, since the currency is not centralized.

Security from Cyber Threats

Cryptocurrency is an entity that has taken shape solely in the digital landscape. Herein lies its most beneficial yet dangerous attribute: this form of currency is the least protected from cybercrimes and hackers. You are out there on your own, while you decide to invest and hold on to cryptocurrency. Risks of your account being hacked into are high, and to make matters worse, conventional channels of dispute resolution are of no use.

Market Value Fluctuations

As mentioned earlier, the value of cryptocurrency is not pegged directly to any specific market. That is not to say that it is free from value fluctuations. On the contrary, speculation-based trading is indeed very high, and the value is often based on the perceived levels of acceptance of this currency. What this means is that your investment could lose half its value overnight without any concrete reason to warrant that depreciation.

Taxation

In the United States, the IRS considers cryptocurrencies like Bitcoin, etc. as property, for taxation purposes. Moreover, at present, this form of currency is not acceptable as a part of a tax-qualified IRA. Hence, there are no legal solutions to shield it from being fully taxed.

Keeping Your Digital Codes Safe

Keeping your digital codes safe is crucial if you are going to be involved in cryptocurrency in any way. Your digital codes, be it your passwords, keys, etc. are akin to the key to your bank locker.

These can give someone access to all your fortune and hard work very easily. Therefore, it should be important, that you take care of these digital codes carefully. It should not be written out so that the outside world can peek into it.

Furthermore, like your cryptocurrency wallet, your private key is your only hope of accessing and making use of your cryptocurrency. If you lose your private key, you cannot recover it, and your account as well as the money inside it may be lost. Therefore, make sure that you have your digital codes securely with you, and you do not lose them in any case.

Cryptocurrency and the Darknet

If you are not familiar with the darknet, it is the anonymous region of the Internet filled with all sorts of content and markets that cannot operate legally on the open regulated Internet we access.

This darknet is accessed through secure proxy-based browsers, like the Tor browser. You can find everything imaginable on the darknet, no matter how punishable it may be by law.

The darknet hosts a lot of markets that deal with drugs, arms trafficking, etc. Since these markets wish to stay anonymous and untraceable from the law, all the transactions that are made there are made through cryptocurrency.

Therefore, you need to ascertain that your cryptocurrency account is not used for any such transactions. Law enforcement works hard in trying to catch up to people who operate these markets, and to the customers who reach out to these markets. Therefore, make sure that your account and its cryptocurrency amount are only used for safe transactions.

CHAPTER 6:

Blockchain Introduction

What Is Blockchain?

To summarize what blockchain is, nothing like a quote from mathematician Jean-Paul Delahaye, who describes it as "a huge notebook, that everyone can read freely and for free, on which everyone can write, but which is impossible to erase and indestructible."

Blockchain is a technology that makes it possible to carry out transactions (such as payments) and transmit information (contracts, sales) in a secure manner and without an intermediary (bank, credit institution, etc.). The resulting information is stored in chronological order and time-stamped. When a set of operations is saved, the previous set of operations becomes unalterable, and so on. Thus, all the transactions recorded on the blockchain, as they are passed, are kept, viewable by all network participants, and tamper-proof.

There are many types of blockchains. Two of them are particularly popular: the one with the so-called "Proof of Work" consensus and the "Proof of Stake" consensus. To function, blockchains need validators, that is to say, entities that will check the register of operations that have taken place on the network.

Blockchain can be applied in other industries apart from cryptocurrencies.

Introduction to Blockchain Technology

One of the first terms you'll hear when delving into the world of cryptocurrencies is "blockchain." To understand Bitcoin, cryptocurrencies in general, and the future of decentralized computing, it is critical to understand the principles of blockchain technology. So, what is the blockchain and why is it important?

The blockchain is the framework, or "protocol," on which Bitcoin functions, as well as many other cryptocurrencies and emerging technologies. Essentially, a blockchain can be thought of *as* a public ledger that is distributed across many computers throughout the world. Each Bitcoin transaction that happens is recorded and added to the blockchain, as a new "block," and linked to the previous transaction with a special timestamp, like a link in a long "chain."

The blockchain is managed through a distributed, peer-to-peer network, meaning that it is stored and updated continuously across many different computers all over the world. Anybody can run the software to turn their computer into a "node" in this giant network, helping to maintain this ongoing record of transactions. This distributed model means that a bunch of different copies of the blockchain exist all across the globe, which makes it essentially impossible for anyone to manipulate transaction information once it has been recorded.

Secure By Design

To help visualize the blockchain a bit more clearly, it is useful to imagine Fort Knox. Famously, Fort Knox houses the gold bullion depository for the United States. A boatload of gold is stored deep within Fort Knox. To keep this gold safe, Fort Knox employs armed guards, blast-proof vaults, and lots of other hardcore onsite security measures. If gold needs to be transferred, we can imagine armored vehicles and soldiers with machine guns keeping watch while the gold is moved. For a criminal to break into Fort Knox and steal the gold would be extremely difficult, not only because of the fortified compound but also because gold, itself, is a heavy physical substance that would be difficult to move.

Banks (and many other institutions) have historically emulated a similar model when trying to protect assets, storing everything in centralized locations that rely on layers of security measures. Today, however, the vast majority of financial information exists digitally, in the form of data. We trust that banks have the cash to back up the numbers we see in our bank accounts, but for the majority of people at any given time, those numbers are a record of value, rather than a physical cash amount stashed in a vault.

Each block in the blockchain is linked to the previous block and recorded publicly across many different nodes all over the world. Rather than breaking into one central server and stealing or manipulating data, in order for someone such as a hacker to alter the blockchain, they would have to change the information not only one block but on the entire blockchain, simultaneously, across the majority of the computers that store it all across the globe.

Technically speaking, this would require such a massive amount of computing power that it would be effectively impossible to accomplish under current conditions. This lack of centralized data storage makes the blockchain system secure by design. If somebody does try to enter a false transaction, for example by sending themselves Bitcoins that don't exist, the many different computers that maintain the blockchain will see that the math does not add up. If the math doesn't add up, the transaction will be deemed invalid and rejected, so it will not be added to the record on the blockchain.

The Future of Blockchain

While blockchain technology is still in a nascent enough stage that virtually anything can happen, there are a number of things that are being worked on at a governmental level that should be considered in the context of your future usage.

More Control

As previously mentioned, one of the biggest benefits of a blockchain is its ability to function completely autonomously. However, due to the fact that bitcoin then allowed for near-anonymous transactions, it made it very easy for those with an interest in avoiding the law to do so. As cryptocurrency becomes more well-known, regulatory and governmental agencies including the Securities and Exchange Commission, Department of Homeland Security, FBI, and the Financial Crimes Enforcement Network, just in the US, have all started becoming more interested in its potential for unlawful activities.

The scrutiny began to increase during 2013 when the Financial Crimes Enforcement Network decided that cryptocurrency exchanges represented a form of an existing money service business. This meant that they would then fall under government regulations. DHS quickly took advantage of this fact to freeze the accounts of Mt. Gox, the biggest bitcoin exchange in the world at this time based on accusations of money laundering.

This was then followed up with a more recent SEC ruling to deny bitcoin the ability to open an official cryptocurrency exchange-traded fund. This move led to a decrease in the price of bitcoin, though that decrease was then countered by an even stronger increase. The denial of this application was still pending review as of September 2017. This then places cryptocurrencies into a bit of an odd situation as their increasing levels of scrutiny make it harder for them to follow through on their purpose, despite being more popular than ever.

If cryptocurrency is ever going to reach a truly mainstream level, and be absorbed into existing financial systems then it needs to find a way to remain true to its initial purpose while also becoming complex enough to hold off the security threats it is sure to face in the future. What's more, it will also need to become simple enough that the average person can use it without issue. Finally, it would need to remain decentralized enough to still be recognizable, while also including various checks and balances to prevent misuse when it comes to things like money laundering or tax evasion. Taken together, this makes it likely that the successful blockchain of the future is going to be some sort of amalgamation of the current form and a more traditional currency.

United States

The United States government is currently working hard to crack down on those who are using blockchain as a means to launder money. They aren't going to be content with that level of control for long, it seems, as signs point to the fact that they are currently working on their own blockchain-based cryptocurrency known as Fedcoin. The idea here is that the Federal Reserve could generate a unique cryptocurrency quite easily. The only difference between the blockchain they create and any other is the fact that it would allow for the Federal Reserve to retain the power to go in and remove transactions that they don't approve of.

The rollout of the Fedcoin would occur after the genesis block was created and the rate of Fedcoins being set to 1 to 1 with the dollar. Over time, it would become more and more difficult to come across regular dollars until they were phased out entirely. This would then ultimately lead to a type of cryptocurrency that is both decentralized for its individual transactions, and centralized when it comes to things like limiting available supply and keeping an eye on all types of transactions.

Blockchain Uses

It has proven to be helpful and, above all, revolutionary in various industries, the first of all in Finance, but it has also entered the world of medicine, insurance, or education very hard. With the following examples, you will see how Blockchain is changing the world as we know it:

Blockchain in the Insurance Industry

In not long, data storage using Blockchain technology in the insurance industry will become the new standard. This technology's high security and the ability to eliminate fraud and redundancy of policy information make blockchain the natural choice for the insurance industry.

One of the most exciting points of blockchain technology is the possibility of generating smart contracts that could automatically approve or reject any claim for an insurance policy.

Blockchain in Finance/Banking

Indeed the most popular applications are in this sector since blockchain technology can manage many processes that will truly revolutionize banking as we know it. Here you can read an excellent excerpt from the essay on the evolution of finances by Alex Tapscott and Don Tapscott for the Harvard Business Review

"Money, stocks, bonds, securities, deeds, contracts, and practically all other types of assets can be moved and stored safely, privately and peer-to-peer, because trust is not established by powerful intermediaries such as banks and governments, but instead by network consensus, cryptography, collaboration, and smart code."

As cryptocurrencies gain popularity, major economic powers such as China will take steps to adopt digital currency. In short, Blockchain can revolutionize our financial system and eliminate the need for so many intermediary companies, which only lengthen and make them more expensive.

Blockchain and Medicine

It helps manage data and automate processes in an industry where precision is a matter of life and death. In the US, a medical error is one of the most common causes of death. Storing records on a blockchain would reduce redundancies and errors that lead to those deaths.

Blockchain also enables greater precision in pharmaceutical medication, which would help patients prevent the diversion of opiates to illegal markets.

Blockchain and Logistics

In the supply chains and logistics industries, blockchain makes it easier to track the location of commodities as they are produced, packaged, and distributed to various points of sale. Smart Contracts allow payments and authorizations to be made through the products' GPS location; this aspect would increase the efficiency in this industry for an approximate value of 1,500 million dollars.

Blockchain and Real Estate

In this industry, blockchain is increasing the efficiency of real estate transactions, reducing the time it takes to check the financial information of each of those involved, thus improving transparency in the industry. All of this would help make document forgeries or rental scams virtually impossible, rendering all property-related transactions incorruptible.

Blockchain and Education

In education, blockchain technology will help standardize the verification of certificates issued by learning institutions. It can also be guaranteed that all educators' credentials are valid. Redundancies would be eliminated, and errors in student performance data would be avoided.

Blockchain in Marketing

The applications, in this case, are very diverse, and as a consequence, the industry will improve precision when choosing its target consumers. For the benefit of consumers themselves, transparency will increase considerably.

Blockchain will ensure that people are not overexposed to certain advertising pieces or even get people automatically paid for using their data.

It will be possible to verify that the followers of a brand are people and not bots. The legitimacy of sponsored contests can be guaranteed, ensuring only one vote per participant.

Blockchain and Business

As you can imagine, the applications of blockchain technology in business are infinite, from improving the accuracy or transparency of records to eliminating administrative processes that ultimately hinder efficiency. There is still a long way to go to discover and, above all, to optimize. But financial experts are completely confident that we will see full adoption of this technology in industries in no time.

It is important to understand the concept behind blockchain and how it applies to your industry because it is the future.

CHAPTER 7:

All Cryptocurrencies

Ethereum (ETH)

In the long run, Ethereum holds much more promise than Bitcoin. While the two competing cryptocurrencies both rely on blockchain technology, they have major differences in terms of objective and capability. Bitcoin is strictly a payment system, which is only one application of blockchain technology. Instead of focusing on one use as Bitcoin did, Ethereum allows developers to build all kinds of decentralized apps. This means that Ethereum has the capability of revolutionizing all services and sectors that are currently centralized. Today, there are two parallel Ethereum blockchains, Ethereum (ETH) and Ethereum Classic (ETC). Ethereum Classic was introduced after a split that came following the hacking of the Ethereum-based DAO project in September of 2016, where about $50 million Ether was stolen.

Litecoin (LTC)

One of the major changes that Lee made was the cryptographic "hash" function used by Litecoin. Unlike Bitcoin which uses the SHA256 hash, Lee introduced "scrypt" in Litecoin. Switching to scrypt allowed Litecoin to process and confirm transactions faster. Litecoin transactions are verified in about two minutes, while Bitcoin might take up to 10 minutes to verify transactions. Another advantage of using "scrypt" is that it allowed users with consumer-grade CPUs to mine for coins, unlike Bitcoin which requires miners to have CPUs that are specialized for mining.

By doing so, Lee gave Litecoin more liquidity, since there are more coins available for purchase, preventing the hoarding that has become so common with Bitcoin buyers. Another major difference between Litecoin and Bitcoin is that Litecoin uses a slightly different mining protocol, which allows a fairer distribution of mined coins.

Litecoin also allows for faster testing and implementation of new technology. For instance, Litecoin pioneered and implemented SegWit (Segregated Witness) technology way before Bitcoin. All in all, Litecoin is a strong cryptocurrency with a good reputation and solid economic principles.

IOTA (IOT)

IOTA includes things like internet-enabled cars, computers, kitchen appliances, microchips, home automation devices, hospital devices, and so on. By being the backbone of IOT, IOTA aims to achieve its call of being the "Ledger of Everything." Apart from being the backbone of IOT, IOTA was also developed to solve some of the challenges faced by Bitcoin, including issues of scalability, speed, and transaction fees. IOTA has one key difference from other cryptocurrencies like Bitcoin. With blockchain-based cryptocurrencies, the network of computers needs to verify a transaction before it is completed. With the Tangle, verification does not rely on the network. Instead, the Tangle relies on a system that requires the sender to perform some proof of work before they can make their transaction. By doing so, the sender approves two transactions, thereby combining the transaction and its verification. Since it is up to the sender to provide the proof of work, there is no need for miners. This has two benefits. First, by eliminating miners, the Tangle makes IOTA fully decentralized. Instead of having players who have an effect on the network without actually using it (miners simply enable the network, but they do not use it), the IOTA network is maintained solely by the "users" who are actually making transactions. Second, by having the sender approve two transactions before they can make their transaction, this system makes the IOTA protocol faster. It also means that an increase in the number of users leads to a faster validation speed. This is unlike what normally happens with other cryptocurrencies like Bitcoin, where an increase in the number of users slows down the validation time. Since there are no miners, users do not have to pay any fees for maintaining the network either.

Ripple (XRP)

Unlike many cryptocurrencies out there, Ripple was not built as a variant of Bitcoin. Instead, its developers built it from scratch and incorporated some major changes in its architecture. Unlike most cryptocurrencies which use a proof-of-stake or proof-of-work system to verify transactions, Ripple uses a unique consensus system, where the computers in the network keep monitoring any changes. Once a majority of the computers in the network observe a transaction, it is added to the public ledger. The consensus system has a number of advantages over the proof-of-work or proof-of-stake systems. Transactions verified under the consensus system are validated faster and require less processing power. While it might seem possible for hackers to compromise the consensus system, it is designed in such a way that any unreliable results are rejected by the network.

Since the Ripple network is meant to facilitate cross-currency conversions, Ripples can be exchanged for a wide range of fiat currencies and altcoins. Some businesses also allow customers to exchange Ripples for air miles and reward points. Unlike altcoins, like Ether and Litecoin, which are sold on cryptocurrency exchanges, you have to go through Ripple Gateways to buy Ripples. The Gateways work in the same way PayPal works.

Dash (Dash)

Dash is a cryptocurrency that was developed by Evan Duffield and Kyle Hagan. Launched in 2014, it was originally known as Darkcoin. After a year in existence, it rebranded to Dash, which is the shortened version of "digital cash." By developing

Dash, Kyle and Evan wanted to create a cryptocurrency that is totally secret and anonymous. Most cryptocurrencies are not thoroughly anonymous. Though addresses are not linked to personally identifiable information, the network knows the number of coins within each address and anyone can keep track of coins as they move from one address to another. This makes it possible for someone to independently know the identity of those users who do not take measures to protect their identity. To keep users anonymous, Dash uses a decentralized master code network which makes Dash transactions practically impossible to trace.

The high level of anonymity offered by Dash is enabled by a system known as Darksend. With this system, specialized computers known as master codes collect several transactions and execute them simultaneously, thereby keeping the transaction untraceable. It becomes impossible to track the source and destination of the coins. To make your transactions even more anonymous, you can choose to have the master codes mix your transaction for multiple rounds before completing the transaction. To maintain this anonymity, the Dash ledger is not publicly accessible. The high level of anonymity has also prevented wide acceptance by businesses.

Another distinguishing feature of Dash is its hashing algorithm. Instead of using the SHA256 or scrypt hash, Dash uses a unique X11 hash which requires lesser processing power, allowing users with consumer-grade CPUs to mine for Dash coins. Other notable advantages of Dash include its speedy transaction verification (4 seconds) and low transaction fees. However, the fees are likely to rise once more people join the network. Dash also has a voting system in place to allow the quick implementation of important changes.

Monero (XMR)

Monero is another cryptocurrency that, just like Dash, is focused on privacy and anonymity. Monero was launched in 2014 by a team of seven programmers, five of whom chose to remain anonymous. Due to its anonymity features, it quickly gained popularity with cryptocurrency enthusiasts. Like most other cryptocurrencies, Monero is completely open-source. The development of the platform is driven by the community and donations. This technique is a digital version of group signatures. Each transaction on the Monero network is enshrouded by a group of cryptographic signatures. This way, it is impossible to pinpoint the actual sender or recipient in the transaction. Even with a person's wallet address, it is impossible to see the number of coins in the wallet or keep track of where they are spent. This means that it is impossible for Monero coins to become tainted, as a result of any previous dubious transactions.

Monero transactions are verified using the same proof-of-work system that Bitcoin uses. However, a major difference between Bitcoin and Monero is that while Bitcoin block sizes are limited at 2MB, there is no limitation on Monero block sizes. The lack of limited block sizes presents the risk of malicious miners using disproportionately huge blocks to clog up the system.

Neo (NEO)

NEO is a Chinese cryptocurrency that was founded by Erik Zhang and Da Hongfei. NEO is designed to be a smart economy platform, much like Ethereum. It has even been referred to as "China's Ethereum." NEO first launched under the name *Antshares*. In August 2017, it rebranded to NEO Smart Contract Economy. NEO's objective is very similar to that of Ethereum. NEO provides a platform where developers can develop decentralized applications and deploy smart contracts. Unlike Ethereum, which only supports its Solidity programming language, NEO can be used with common programming languages such as C#, Python, and Java. Since consensus under the dBFT system only needs to be achieved by a subset of the network, this system requires less processing power and allows the network to handle a higher transaction volume. NEO claims that it is capable of handling over 1,000 transactions per second, whereas Ethereum only handles 15 transactions per second. The dBFT system also eliminates the possibility of a hard fork, which makes NEO a great option for digitizing real-world financial assets.

Bitcoin (BTC)

New Bitcoins are created as a reward for mining, which is what keeps the Bitcoin protocol running. The Bitcoin protocol is configured in a way that keeps the rate of production of new Bitcoins around a certain average. If more processing power is deployed to mine for new Bitcoins, mining becomes harder. If some processing power is taken from the network, the difficulty of mining new Bitcoins decreases. The protocol was created with a limit of 21 million Bitcoins, after which no more Bitcoins will be released.

Bitcoin can be divided into smaller units known as MilliBitcoins, MicroBitcoins, and Satoshis. The smallest unit of Bitcoin is first-ever the Satoshi (0.00000001), which was named after the mysterious inventor of Bitcoin. As the modern cryptocurrency, Bitcoin is the easiest to get and enjoys the widest acceptance.

OmiseGO (OMG)

OmiseGO is a cryptocurrency that has gained a lot of popularity from cryptocurrency enthusiasts lately. Launched in 2013, it is an interesting yet very ambitious project which aims to use Ethereum-based financial technology to un-bank the banked. OmiseGO is currently built on the Ethereum platform as an ERC20-token, though it will eventually launch its own blockchain. OmiseGO's vision is to become the leading P2P cryptocurrency exchange platform. Instead of being just an altcoin, OmiseGO is built to act as a financial platform with the aim of disrupting the financial sector as we currently know it.

OmiseGO intends to solve a challenge that most cryptocurrency exchanges have failed to address. To purchase a cryptocurrency in most cryptocurrency exchanges, you have to start with a fiat currency. To exchange one altcoin for another, you have to convert the altcoins to fiat currency or Bitcoin, and then convert the fiat currency/Bitcoin to your desired altcoins. Throughout this process, the exchange charges fees for each transaction. This means that you will pay fees to convert altcoins to fiat currency/Bitcoin, and then pay fees again to convert the fiat currency/Bitcoin to other altcoins.

OmiseGO plans to solve this problem by linking all existing cryptocurrency wallets to a central OmiseGO Blockchain. This way, users can easily exchange altcoins for other altcoins without having to convert them to fiat currency or Bitcoin. This means that instead of multiple fees, users will pay a one-time fee.

OmiseGO also aims to bring decentralization to cryptocurrency exchanges. Currently, most exchanges are centralized operations. The records of all transactions as well as data about different users are stored in databases that are stored on the company's servers. OmiseGO aims to decentralize the exchange functionality by having all the transaction info and user data stored on the blockchain. This way, the data is more secure, since a hacker would then need to perform a 51% attack (gaining control over 51% of the computers in the network) in order to breach the blockchain, which is virtually impossible.

NEM (XEM)

NEM is a revolutionary cryptocurrency that was launched in March 2015. Unlike many other cryptocurrencies which were created as variants of existing projects, NEM was built from the ground up, with its own unique source code. NEM derived its name from the New Economic Movement, the group which came up with cryptocurrency. NEM is designed as a blockchain-based technology that can be customized to fit different business purposes. At the core of NEM's protocol is what is known as the "Smart Asset System."

Since NEM can be customized to fit multiple use cases, it has unlimited potential uses. It can be used as a central ledger in the banking sector, a means of keeping secure records, a blockchain-based voting system, an escrow service, a means of rewarding points in loyalty programs, a crowdfunding platform, as a means of stock ownership, and so on. This shows how much potential NEM holds.

Unlike most cryptocurrency platforms, NEM has a messaging platform. It also has a reward system and supports multisignature transactions. One of the key differences between NEM and other cryptocurrencies is the verification method. Instead of proof-of-work or proof-of-stake systems, NEM relies on a unique proof-of-importance system, where block calculation chances are allocated based on the contribution of a user to the development/distribution of the platform. Users who make a lot of contributions get rewarded with more chances. This allows a fair distribution of mining chances among users.

The NEM network is fast, with a transaction verification wait time of about one minute. This means that you can rely on NEM to make instant global money transfers. With the proof-of-importance system, users do not need expensive hardware to mine NEM coins.

CHAPTER 8:

Wallets

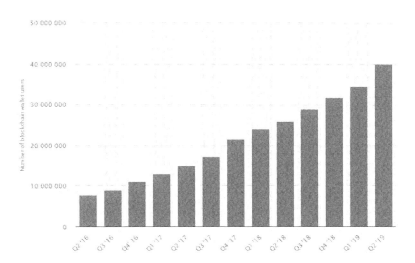

What Is a Cryptocurrency Wallet?

Many people think that a cryptocurrency wallet is where we keep our digital cash, or electronic cash safe and secured, and it's somewhat true, yet there are a lot more into that. First and foremost, back in the day when Satoshi Nakamoto came up with the solution for wallet, it was actually called "client," not a wallet. But for everyone's convenience, the nickname was quickly invented which is nowadays only know as a wallet or cryptocurrency wallet. In the old traditional financial system, when it comes to cash like paper money, we normally keep that in the wallet, or at least we used to, but when it comes to cryptocurrencies, there are no coins in the cryptocurrency wallet whatsoever. This is one of the most common misconceptions, that people believe they have all their cryptocurrencies in their wallets. This is not true of course.

How does a Cryptocurrency Wallet work?

In this chapter, I will explain how a cryptocurrency wallet works. As I mentioned wallets are a software technology, and each cryptocurrency wallets have a private key as well as a public key, but what I didn't mention yet, is that each wallet also has is a password. First of all, it doesn't matter what cryptocurrency we talk about, as each coin has its own official release of wallets. For example, Bitcoin has a bitcoin wallet, Ethereum has an Ethereum wallet, Dash has a dash wallet, and so on, but there are also third-party wallets, released by other companies, and those could be all sorts of wallets, which could be named something else, other than the actual cryptocurrency they would hold access to. Third-party wallet brands are for example Bred Wallet, Exodius, Jaxx, and so on, which I will talk about later. But for now, what you need to know is that all wallets are having the same functionality when it comes to private keys and public keys. In order to better understand what these keys represent, I will provide an example of an e-mail, and instead of comparing it to a general wallet, I will specifically take an example of a bitcoin wallet. For example in the case of an e-mail, you have an e-mail address, which you can send and receive e-mails to and from. This e-mail address would represent the public key of your Bitcoin wallet. Bitcoin public keys can be provided to anyone when you wish to receive a payment, and if you send someone a payment, they will see your public key is where they have received the funds. So basically your public key can be online, and you can show it to anyone, similarly to your e-mail address, when it comes to e-mails. When it comes to Bitcoin addresses, they are most times 34 characters long and consist of random digits of uppercase and lowercase letters. Bitcoin public addresses always start with 1, and never consist of an uppercase of O, or a number 0.

Mobile Wallets

First and foremost, there are many different kinds of mobile wallets and Blockchain.info has one as well. Blockchain.info provides both; online and mobile wallets too. On the other hand, there are many mobile wallets that exist, which are specifically invented for cell phones only. Having a mobile wallet is essential for making payments anywhere you go, as your cell phone probably will be on you most of the time. Mobile wallets are great to check your account anytime pretty much anywhere where you have internet access. Mobile wallets can provide decent security too; but you must back up your mobile wallet, same as your desktop wallet. For example, if you were to lose your phone or break it, buying another phone and having backup phrases to your private keys, you can simply back up your new cell phone as nothing happened. Nevertheless, if you don't back up your mobile wallet, you can lose access to all your bitcoins forever.

Hot Wallets

They are connected to the Internet in some way. For instance, a lot of cryptocurrency exchanges as well provide users with a wallet feature.

They will be able to transfer the cryptocurrency, assuming a hacker is able to find its way into someone's exchange account.

In addition, the hackers could loot the cryptocurrency as well, assuming the exchange itself is hacked.

Another common type of hot wallet is called a 'software wallet' that is hosted as a program on your computer.

Cold Wallet

They are not connected to the Internet and they're technically safer compare to hot wallets. For instance, a lot of cryptocurrency exchanges that hold large amounts of cryptocurrency tend to store most of the cryptocurrency in offline cold wallets to minimize the damage assuming a hack were to take place.

(CWs)Cold wallets contain hardware wallets that are essentially little plastic devices particularly designed for storing someone's private key safe.

Another common type of cold wallet is known as a paper wallet that is just your private key printed (or put down) on a sheet of paper.

(ETFA) Enabling Two-Factor Authentication (and Google Authenticator)

Keep in mind that, most cryptocurrency like Bitcoin can't be "hacked" in the sense that anybody can be able to control its programming as they so desire.

Nevertheless, the locations that keep private keys safe are really within reach of being hacked.

CHAPTER 9:

Bitcoin mining

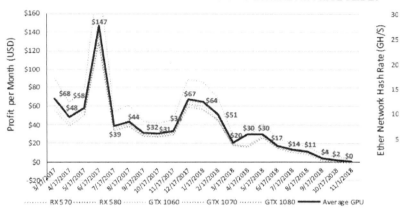

PROFITABILITY OF MINING WITH GPUS FALLS AS ETHEREUM PRICE SLIDES

Y ou may have heard the term "mining" used with regards to Bitcoin. In this episode, we'll look at what mining is, how it works, whether it is profitable and how to mine Bitcoin.

What is mining?

Mining is the process of adding blocks to the block chain and creating new bitcoins. For each block attached to the block chain, new bitcoins are created that are paid as a reward to the computer that combines the block to the block chain.

Getting this reward for adding a block to the block chain is compared to mining small gems out of a large piece of rock, there is a lot of work, chipping away at a large block to gain a little reward for all the effort.

A miner is a computer connected to the Bitcoin block chain network that solves a puzzle to add a block to the block chain. The miner that successfully solves a mystery can add a new block to the block chain and is rewarded in Bitcoin for their effort, this is known as the block reward.

The puzzle that the miners are trying to solve is challenging to explain, but easy to confirm it is correct once the answer has been found. This is a combination to a lock, it is difficult to guess, but once the mixture to the lock is found, other people can enter that combination number and confirm it opens the lock.

How does mining work?

When a transaction is sent on the Bitcoin network, it remains as pending until it is added to a block on the system. Miners connected to the Bitcoin network can select any of the pending transactions to be included in a neighborhood. Usually, they will choose the operations with the highest transaction fees, as they receive the transaction fees along with the block reward.

A block can only be added to the network if it has a valid hash number below the current network target. The puzzle that the miners are trying to solve is finding a name that creates a hash that is lower than the network target.

This can be thought of like rolling a dice, the network target might be 4, so if you move a number lower than 4, you can add a valid block to the block chain and receive the block reward. Skill does not play a factor in running a smaller number; it is pure chance.

The Bitcoin network is designed to add a block to the block chain every 10 minutes, as more miners join the system, they increase the chance that the number they guess will be below the network target.

In the dice example, if it takes one person 10 minutes to roll a number below four then another person joins the network, then, in theory, it will halve the time taken. The Bitcoin network adjusts by decreasing the network target to 2 which increases the difficulty. Now they have to roll a number below two before it is considered below the network target and they can add a block to the block chain.

Once a valid block is added to the block chain, all the miners repeat this process for the next group of transactions to add another compelling block to the block chain. The Bitcoin network does this on a much larger scale, with hundreds of thousands of computers randomly guessing numbers to create a hash number that is lower than the network target. Every 2,016 blocks the network target is adjusted to ensure blocks are being added every 10 minutes.

Bitcoin Mining Profit Calculator

This platform is a great way to start if you're completely new to the world of crypto and the concept of Bitcoin in general. It's not just a trading simulator. It gives you a complete introduction to the concept of Bitcoin and what it means for the global economy. An introduction like such is essential if you're entering the market for the first time.

Understanding how this website works is simple. It's an interactive clicker game which is purely fictional. The website will update with explanations and updates as the game carries on and you click on the various prompts that show up on the screen. These will allow you to make difference choices which will ultimately decide how successful you'll be as a day trader. Since the crypto world can be unpredictable, the game embraces the uncertainty completely and ensures you understand how the crypto trading world works.

The game also makes sure that you don't miss out on any kind of information. The prompts that keep coming up in the game will educated you on the different factors that affects the price of Bitcoin. It will also educate you on the different workings of the Bitcoin community. Even though you won't make money with the help of this website, it will equip you with the mindset you'll need when you eventually step foot into the actual crypto trading market.

Bitcoin Hero

This platform is for people who already have an understanding of how the crypto trading world works. Bitcoin Hero is a brilliant choice for people who have been trying their luck in the crypto market and haven't been lucky. To ensure that this platform is suitable for people on every platform, it can be used on both mobile and PC. There's also no need to install the app on to your phone, but if you don't want to open your browser application every time you want to use it, you can also download the app which is available of both iOS and Android.

While downloading the application isn't necessary, it does have the important feature which allows you to track your progress over several sessions of trading. When you start on the platform, you have $10,000 in your account and you can buy or sell four cryptocurrencies, which are:

- Bitcoin,
- Ethereum,
- Litecoin, and
- Dash

The best part is that the prices of these currencies are imported from the real world so there's a genuine unpredictability factor. Because of this, you can catch up on how trends prevail in the industry without the risk of losing money.

Proof-of-work

The process of randomly guessing numbers to create a valid hash and add a block to block chain is known as "Proof-of-work." It takes a significant amount of electricity and computing power during the process, so a valid hash acts as proof that work was completed and resources such as computing power and electricity were contributed to the network.

The computing power of the Bitcoin network is over 10,000 times more powerful than the world's 500 most influential supercomputers combined. Given the computing power of the Bitcoin network, there is criticism that resources are wasted in a process that is primarily randomly guessing numbers.

Other cryptocurrencies use alternative methods such as "proof-of-stake," "proof-of-burn," "proof-of-activity" and "proof-of-capacity."

Mining and security

The more miners the Bitcoin network has, the more secure it theoretically is. Bitcoin is a decentralized network and all computers connected to the network have access to the block chain.

Whenever a transaction occurs, it is updated across all computers on the network. Any computer can add a block to the blockchain, but the majority of computers on the network must accept it as valid.

To control a decentralized network, over 50% of the computing power of the web would need to be managed. The more miners and computing power contributed to the system, the more difficult the system is to control. It is almost wholly unfeasible to control over 50% of the computers on the Bitcoin network.

Is mining profitable?

The simple answer is "no," Bitcoin mining is no longer profitable on a home computer.

The difficulty of Bitcoin mining has increased, and there are companies with access to cheap electricity running thousands of computers all mining Bitcoin. This makes it unfeasible to mine on a home computer profitably.

Mining requires a significant amount of electricity and top of the range mining specific computer chips, known as ASICs. Even with free heat, it would take a very long time to recover the initial costs of buying the computer equipment to mine bitcoins.

Mining Pools

If you have a mining specific computer card and access to free/cheap electricity you can combine your computing power into a mining pool. A mining pool combines the computing power of small computers making them work together to mine Bitcoin.

This still requires a fast computer chip or mining specific chips and electricity however it allows individuals or smaller miners to combine resources to compete against more significant mining operations. There is a range of Bitcoin mining pools. However it does take some technical knowledge to set up a computer to mine and connect it to a mining pool.

There are mining profitability calculators online, that show the potential profits based on computer speed and electricity costs.

Mining other cryptocurrencies and trading for Bitcoin

While Bitcoin mining is very competitive and not profitable, it may be possible to mine other cryptocurrencies and then exchange them for bitcoins.

Some websites show the profitability and difficult of certain mining cryptocurrencies. If a cryptocurrency has a low difficulty and high profitability, these cryptocurrencies could be mined and then exchanged for bitcoins.

There are also cryptocurrencies such as Story that pay for hard drive space instead of computing power. If you have spare hard drive space, you may be able to earn cryptocurrencies by renting out your hard drive space and then trading that for bitcoins.

Cloud Mining

Cloud mining is where computing power is purchased from a large mining company that has existing computers mining bitcoins. They have access to cheap electricity and large numbers of fast computer chips already mining.

Cloud mining saves on set-up costs such as purchasing equipment and reduces the ongoing costs such as electricity.

There may still be current maintenance fees however these are taken out of the bitcoins before they are paid out to you. They also offer the opportunity to mine more profitable cryptocurrencies and exchange them for bitcoins.

Cloud mining is potentially much more profitable than mining on a home computer connected to a mining pool. However, even with cloud mining the profitability is still not guaranteed, and many factors impact profitability.

While the mining reward for a block may be significant, most people are unable to mine a block by themselves. They have to combine computing power in a mining pool or through cloud mining. The mining rewards received through cloud mining or mining pools for each person contributing computing power is very small. It does accumulate over time, however, some wallets and exchanges won't accept mining rewards to be paid to them as it will result in too many small transactions to process.

Before connecting to a mining pool or beginning cloud mining, make sure your wallet can accept mining rewards.

CHAPTER 10:

Various coin base

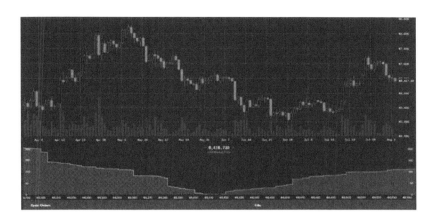

Best exchanges to buy cryptocurrencies

Coinbase is undoubtedly one of the best Exchange platforms. It gained sudden popularity as people tested the service on mobile after launching the mobile app for IOS and Android. Coinbase is an American service, and as such, it has quite strict rules in terms of identification. It is necessary to send a lot of personal data, including an identity document photographed front and back. The fees are quite low, and in addition to being an excellent exchange, it also offers a functional online wallet service.

Kraken

Kraken has now become an excellent exchange, so much so that many sites recommend it to its readers. It allows the exchange of many currency pairs and the best crypto of the moment. The strong point is on the commissions applied to operate, reaching a maximum value of 0.26%. Particular attention to the security profile with specific account verification and the possibility of making deposits and withdrawals on the online account through a classic bank transfer or creating a cryptocurrency wallet. Limits are also applied to the daily withdrawal and protection of user data with the same offline mode.

Bitpanda

Bitpanda is an integrated platform, which offers, in addition to the exchange, an excellent free wallet service. The platform is liquid and functional for buying and selling both Bitcoin and Ethereum, of which it always has very updated quotes.

The flexibility regarding accepted payment methods is undoubtedly appreciable: Mastercard, Visa and bank transfer, and most of the most famous electronic payment systems. The only flaw is that for the registration and use of the portal, it is necessary to undergo rather strict verification processes, which concern both personal information and the automatic checks of the connection that is established with the site.

Spectrocoin

Spectrocoin allows you to safely exchange four cryptocurrencies: Bitcoin, Dash, Ethereum and NEM. Although some of the most famous are missing, some merits cannot be denied to this service. First of all that of being very functional, both if it is used exclusively as an exchange and by combining the service with the wallet.

Spectrocoin guarantees great anonymity and, not surprisingly, also offers its own prepaid card outside the Visa and Mastercard circuit that can arrive where cryptocurrencies cannot be used.

Binance

Binance was born in 2017, but one year after its foundation, it was already among the 5 most used cryptocurrency exchanges in the world. To date, it has become the best-known service in the world, both for the decidedly wide offer of altcoins (over 500) and for the charisma of its founder, Changpeng Zhao, universally recognized as one of the brightest minds in the sector. There is a US version with a limited number of cryptocurrencies available.

Binance allows you to buy Bitcoin or Ethereum with traditional currency. You can use these two cryptocurrencies to exchange them with all the others on the platform. With a commission of just 0.2% on every cryptocurrency trade, it is also one of the most affordable services in terms of trading costs. It needs verification if you want to trade more than 2 Bitcoins

Bibox

Bibox is one of the latest exchanges to appear on the European market, but... it has recovered well! With a very simple registration and verification procedure, with many currencies to exchange, very low commissions, an interesting ref marketing program and many advantages for old and new customers, it is certainly one of the operators that you should not underestimate.

Poloniex

It is one of the largest exchanges in the United States and specialized above all on Bitcoins' exchange. It does not require you to verify your account to operate online but has limits on maximum withdrawals. Strengths also on commission costs among the lowest present to date and in principle no higher than 0.25%.

The operations to finance the account, on the other hand, can be implemented through the use of a cryptocurrency wallet while preserving the low commission costs.

Bitstamp

It is one of the most quoted platforms for exchanging the best cryptocurrencies in Europe and with the highest volumes in surplus. Its strengths include immediate online execution and acceptance of the main payment methods to fund an account, including credit cards. Attention, also to data security, mainly processed in an off-line manner.

Bittrex

It is among the best and largest cryptocurrency exchanges and with a very wide offer to trade many different currency pairs and on the best crypto of the moment. Its main strength is on the very low commissions and generally set at a level of 0.20% without considering a greater or lesser volume of purchases made. The Bittrex Exchange also requires the verification of the new user's identity with the sending of personal documents and high data protection thanks to a very detailed authentication process that provides for the conservation of the digital assets of this Exchange in offline mode. Furthermore, the deposit and withdrawal operations on the account to operate online concern a personal Wallet with direct access only when users perform transactions. On the Bittrex Exchange, it is also possible to opt for trading operations with altcoins, maintaining anonymity on the operations performed, but with a limit on the number of them that can be selected on the platform.

BitMEX

BitMEX scores numbers that speak for themselves. From mid-2017 onwards, an average of $ 50 billion in value is exchanged and converted into cryptocurrencies on this exchange every month. This service is particularly recommended for those who want to sell Bitcoins and thus convert them into Fiat currency, especially US dollars.

Why? Because the liquidity that BitMEX boasts in the Bitcoin / Dollar cross is 150% higher than the second-ranked platform.

Diversify your portfolio. Do not to invest all your savings in a single currency but to create a portfolio with multiple cryptocurrencies to reduce the positions' total risk.

If you have basic knowledge of statistics, you could try to calculate the correlation between the cryptocurrencies you prefer and then select those with a correlation coefficient as far away from 1, even better if negative.

Two digital currencies are correlated when the trend of their price behaves similarly: if a cryptocurrency price goes up or down, the price of the related will tend to behave in the same way.

Assuming that a crypto in your wallet becomes extremely popular over some time, and its price rises, you will be able to make money even if the other digital currencies perform poorly. Instead, if the currency goes through a negative period, you will cover the losses with the rest's performance.

CHAPTER 11:

Bitcoin and Blockchain

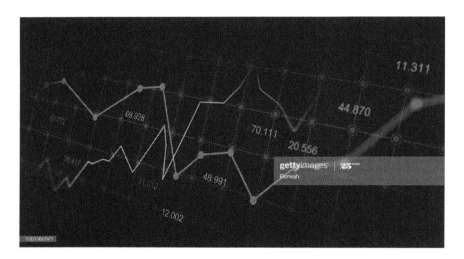

Difference between block chain and bitcoin

Bitcoin was the original use case example of a working block chain, so for years, the two were inseparable because you could not mention block chain without referring to Bitcoin. Block chain was believed to be the only technology behind Bitcoin. However, there is a range of different techniques working together linked to the Bitcoin network and Bitcoin block chain.

The Bitcoin network is mainly used for financial transactions, with these sales recorded on the Bitcoin block chain. The block chain used on the Bitcoin network is just one example of how block chain technology can be used.

With Bitcoin, each block added to the block chain contains a group of financial transactions. However, a block chain can record almost any type of operations or data.

There is a wide range of potential uses being explored for block chain-based systems. The Bitcoin blockchain only records financial transactions, and there are currently no plans for Bitcoin to be used for anything other than digital payments.

Can bitcoins be duplicated or copied like an email?

As bitcoins only exist electronically and can be sent to an email, it is possible to carry the same electronic data twice, the same way you could post the same email more than once. This is known as the double spending problem, which other attempts to create digital currency had struggled to solve until Bitcoin.

While bitcoins only exist electronically and sending bitcoins is like sending an email, they can't be duplicated or copied. In traditional payment systems, there is an intermediary like a bank or Paypal that ensures that electronic currency is not duplicated or double spent. Bitcoin doesn't have an intermediary. However, the majority of the network must agree that transactions are valid. If you send bitcoins to another person, then computers on the network will check that you are authorized to submit those bitcoins or if they have already been spent. If the bitcoins have already been paid, then the transaction will be rejected.

Where are bitcoins held?

When you own bitcoins, they are held in a digital wallet. The wallet doesn't contain bitcoins but contains the public and private keys for accessing and transferring them.

Is Bitcoin anonymous?

Yes, Bitcoin is designed to be mostly anonymous. Any transactions you make on the Bitcoin network, will not show your identity or any information about you.

However, if you are purchasing bitcoins using fiat currencies like U.S dollars, then you will need to set up an account with a company that is regulated the same as other financial institutions.

These regulations will require verification of ID to set up an account and purchase bitcoins with traditional payment methods.

If you purchase bitcoins through a company where you have verified your ID, then transactions from this account can be linked to your identity by the company. These companies are regulated the same way as financial institutions, so if you purchase bitcoins through a company based in the U.S.A then send bitcoins to a bitcoin address in Cuba, Iran or other countries the U.S has financial sanctions on, they will be able to trace this and may cancel your account.

Even if you have a completely anonymous Bitcoin wallet, if you purchase in a store, the store owner will be able to see the address it came from and link that address with your identity.

There are ways to ensure your Bitcoin transactions are anonymous such as using different addresses and wallets. Be aware that it may not be entirely unknown and there may still be regulations you have to comply with.

Is Bitcoin like PayPal?

No, PayPal is an intermediary that allows you to transfer traditional currencies to other people online easily and operates similarly to a conventional bank account with a financial institution. While you can send money to people via PayPal using their email address, it is not the same as throwing cash via Bitcoin. Money transferred via PayPal is in U.S dollars, Euros, and other fiat currencies. Behind the scenes, these transactions are reconciled using internal private ledgers, centralized systems, and traditional bank accounts. Bitcoin is very different as it is an entirely separate currency and payment provider. It operates without government control or any intermediary to process transactions. Transactions are conducted in bitcoins; they are treated by a decentralized network of thousands of computers connected. All deals are published to a public ledger that anyone can view. There are no traditional bank accounts, accountants or centralized internal systems that hold bitcoins or reconcile transactions.

Understanding everything about Blockchain

Everyone has heard of it, but few manage to get a clear idea of what **Blockchain** is. And for a good reason, many books that can be found on the subject are riddled with anglicisms and words taken from the jargon of the stock market and computer scientists. They can easily give the impression that this technology, which is related to Bitcoin and cryptocurrencies, can only be understood by experts.

This revolutionary technology enables rapid peer-to-peer exchange of values or information in complete transparency and without an intermediary. Beyond Bitcoin and the world of cryptocurrencies in general, this concept finds many applications in our daily lives and is expected to gain more importance shortly. This is why it helps understand what it is, how it works, the advantages and disadvantages, and the potential uses.

Peer-to-peer (which we often see in its abbreviated form "P2P") means that the exchange occurs directly from one Internet user to another. Here, no central server: the transfer of data or assets will be done directly from the sender to the receiver.

Blockchain, how does it work?

As we have seen, the blockchain is " a large notebook ", in which the history of all exchanges carried out is kept. The miners/forgers who intervene on the network each have a copy of this register, which can be compared to a database and continuously update it.

All exchanges that have taken place since the creation of the blockchain are logged. Each operation is recorded in a block which groups together several. Put end to end, the blocks form a chain, hence the name blockchain.

In practice, when an operation takes place on the blockchain, the veracity of the information inherent in this operation is guaranteed by a digital signature which results from the alliance of a public key and a private key.

Practical and theoretical applications of blockchain

Besides the cryptocurrency that we all already know, what are the applications of the Blockchain? Yes, contrary to what some suggest, Blockchain (although closely related to Bitcoin and Ethereum) can work in settings other than cryptocurrency. Although in practice, many companies are still hesitant to experiment too much with it.

The supply chain

The application of Blockchain in the supply chain is perhaps one of the most interesting applications of this technology and which would revolutionize this industry, and all the industries that touch it (we will think in particular of the food world, which has been affected by many scandals in recent years; with technology such as Blockchain to ensure tamper-proof monitoring)

Decentralized internet

Although still conceptual, some developers are working on decentralizing the internet using Blockchain technology, thus improving the resilience of the internet in the face of, for example, cyber-attacks.

Decentralized storage in the cloud

While cloud storage currently revolves around centralized companies (like Google), some are playing with the theory of completely decentralized storage that would eliminate the need to rely on large companies that centralize data storage in one place.

Management of intangible assets

The Blockchain represents, above all, a secure and transparent register. Since fraud is almost impossible through the secure system that Blockchain represents, it makes perfect sense that some organizations use this technology to manage intangible assets (e.g., real estate documents when selling a house).

Voting systems

Unfortunately, today we know that any democratic vote can be the victim of attempts to manipulate it to influence the result. Some hypothesize, specifically in electronic voting, that the use of the Blockchain can reduce the number of errors and fraud attempts.

Smart contracts

Although not very widespread, smart contracts are contracts applying computer protocols, thus facilitating their partial or complete self-execution. Blockchain technology could, in theory, make it easier to control these contracts.

Why does Blockchain matter?

It is important because it is one of the safest and most efficient ways to store data sets, especially when different agents use these data for very different purposes. Think about how blockchain is going to change your industry.

Companies pioneering the adoption of Blockchain technology applications are already reaping the benefits of having greater data visibility, integrity, and security. Of course, as Blockchain advances, more and more industries will depend on this technology.

What is Blockchain mining?

Mining is most commonly applied in the vast world of Bitcoin. Mining is the section in which individual "miners" solve computer-generated mathematical problems to add a series of Bitcoin transactions to the public record of their Blockchain; in other words, they generate Bitcoins. Every ten minutes or so, the mining computers collect a few hundred pending

Bitcoin transactions (a 'node') and turn them into a mathematical puzzle.

The first miner to find the solution announces it to others on the network. The other miners then check if the funds' sender has the right to spend the money and if the puzzle's solution is correct. If enough of them give their approval, the block is cryptographically added to the blockchain, and miners move on to the next set of transactions (hence the term "blockchain").

The miner who found the solution receives 6.25 Bitcoins per block as a reward, but only after another 99 blocks have been added to the blockchain. " The rate has decreased over time: it is halved almost every four years since 2009.

Research the market: This is the only guaranteed way of becoming successful. You have to do your research.

Conclusion

Your success as a stock trader will be highly dependent on the effort and time you are willing to invest while learning stock trading as well as rules that apply to this activity. Stock trading is not really complicated, but you may have to some research as we discuss more the mathematical components of this business. For example, you need to learn the difference between an exponential average and a simple average. Other than that, stock trading is less a science and more art.

One of the most common mistakes that most of the new traders are guilty of making is attempting to get rich quickly. Let's say you invested $1,000, and you keep doubling it up with gains for the next 12 months. Following this pattern, you would become a millionaire before the end of one year, right?

A wise investor invests in growth stocks accurately, and afterward sells these stocks after they demonstrate vast share price increments. Rather than clutching them while they descend, the keen investor's like to capitalize on recent gains by selling stocks.

Regardless of whether you invest individually or through a stockbroker, try to remember the significance of selling and stocks effectively and always use technical and fundamentals analysis for stock picking.

Stock trading is not reserved for the ultra-wealthy. Anyone who has enough funds can participate in this game and earn.

It took some effort and time from our end, but you should now a pretty good idea of how you can reach your financial goals without losing all of your money.

Learning about the stock market should not stop with this book. After mastering the concepts here, you should continue to expand your knowledge in investing. There is a lot of books about investments and stock trading out there. You can also dive deeper into the technical analysis as you mature in this trade. ALL THE BEST!

Made in the USA
Middletown, DE
29 September 2021